So you <u>really</u> want

English

2nd Edition

Book One

Susan Elkin

Series Editor: Nicholas Oulton M.A. (Oxon.)

GALORE PARK

www.galorepark.co.uk

Published by ISEB Publications, an imprint of Galore Park Publishing Ltd,
19/21 Sayers Lane, Tenterden, Kent TN30 6BW
www.galorepark.co.uk

Text copyright © Susan Elkin Ltd. 2012

The right of Susan Elkin to be identified as author of this Work has been asserted by her in accordance with sections 77 and 78 of the Copyright, Designs and Patents Act 1988.

Illustrations by Rowan Barnes-Murphy

Design and layout by Qué, Wittersham

Printed by Replika Press Pvt. Ltd, India

ISBN: 978 1 905735 51 8

First printed 2004, new edition September 2012, 2013

An Answer Book is available to accompany this book
ISBN: 978 1 905735 64 8

Details of other Galore Park publications are available at www.galorepark.co.uk

ISEB Revision Guides, publications and examination papers may also be obtained from Galore Park.

Acknowledgements

Since 1968 I have worked with many thousands of pupils and students of all ages in London, Northamptonshire and Kent. From them I have learnt nearly everything I know about how to teach and learn English. In a very real sense this is their book. I thank them all.

I also thank my husband Nicholas Elkin, always the first reader and critic of anything I write. I am indebted to his meticulous eye for detail and his unfailing presence as a sounding board against which I continuously bounce ideas.

Sincere thanks are also due to everyone at Galore Park. This book owes its existence to their hard work and faith in me.

I hope that our combined efforts have eliminated all mistakes. But if any remain they are, of course, mine.

Note to the teacher

This book has been written for pupils preparing for exams at 11+ and meets the standards set by the National Curriculum at Key Stage 2. Each chapter is based around two extracts, one literary and the other from a non-literary source, followed by plenty of ideas to get children writing in as many different styles, moods and modes as there are pupils. The ten chapters, with their supplementary focus on spelling, punctuation, grammar, oracy and wider reading, could provide the basis for a whole year's work in English lessons if whole literary texts were studied as a separate, parallel activity. There are extension tasks in every chapter, too, to stretch pupils who finish quickly or who want (or need) to go further.

Examinations are, however, not education. The real aim of this book is to develop in children the highest possible standards in English – for its own sake – and to make it pleasurable, rigorous and satisfying. I love English and I want users of this book to learn to love it too.

This new edition has several new features designed to broaden the start of the *So you really want to learn* course. Children are asked to read and examine a poem in each chapter, learning about techniques in poetry such as rhyme and assonance along the way. The 'Discuss' exercises should be used to prompt class or group discussions rather than individual written answers. Also new to this edition, the 'Improve your writing' sections (one per chapter) prompt children to practise writing further.

Susan Elkin

Contents

Introduction

The English language 1

Chapter 1 Poor and hungry

The boy who asked for more 5

World hunger 7

Your turn to write 9

Improve your writing 9

'In the Workhouse' 10

Explore poetry further 13

Grammar and punctuation 13

 Full stops 13

 Starting a sentence 13

 Nouns 15

Vocabulary and spelling 16

Speaking and listening 17

Have you read? 18

And if you've done all that ... 18

Chapter 2 In the water

Saved from drowning 19

A mermaid-like sea mammal 21

Your turn to write 22

Improve your writing 23

'The Mermaid' 23

Explore poetry further 25

Grammar and punctuation 26

 Question marks 26

 A spoken question mark 26

 Verbs 27

Vocabulary and spelling 28

Speaking and listening   30

Have you read?   31

And if you've done all that …   31

Chapter 3 Animals

The Elephant's Child   32

Elephants in zoos   37

Your turn to write   38

'Two Performing Elephants'   39

Improve your writing   40

Explore poetry further   41

Grammar and punctuation   42

    Commas for lists   42

    Commas acting as brackets   42

    Adjectives   43

Vocabulary and spelling   44

Speaking and listening   45

Have you read?   46

And if you've done all that …   46

Chapter 4 The Second World War

A discovery   47

Utility clothing   49

Your turn to write   51

Improve your writing   51

'Earlswood'   52

Explore poetry further   55

Grammar and punctuation   55

    Exclamation marks   55

    Adverbs   56

Vocabulary and spelling   57

Speaking and listening   58

Have you read?   59

And if you've done all that …   59

Chapter 5 Shakespeare

Back in time	60
Rebuilding Shakespeare's Globe	63
Your turn to write	64
Improve your writing	65
'Sonnet 91'	65
Explore poetry further	67
Grammar and punctuation	67
Adjectives from nouns	67
Hyphens	68
Dashes	69
Dashes (continued)	70
Vocabulary and spelling	70
Speaking and listening	71
Have you read?	71
And if you've done all that …	72

Chapter 6 Fantasy

The Minotaur	73
Fantastic Mr Fox: a review	75
Your turn to write	77
Improve your writing	78
'Jabberwocky'	79
Explore poetry further	81
Grammar and punctuation	81
Apostrophes	81
Apostrophes (continued)	82
Adjectives for comparing	83
Vocabulary and spelling	84
Speaking and listening	85
Have you read?	86
And if you've done all that …	86

Chapter 7 Dangerous creatures

Shark alert	87
Snap! Moment a camera-shy shark decided enough was enough	89
Your turn to write	90
Improve your writing	91
'The Maldive Shark'	91
Explore poetry further	93
Grammar and punctuation	93
Conjunctions	93
Compound sentences	94
Vocabulary and spelling	95
Speaking and listening	97
Have you read?	97
And if you've done all that …	98

Chapter 8 Traditional tales

Uba-na-ner the magician	99
A traditional Egyptian recipe	102
Your turn to write	103
Improve your writing	104
'Retelling of a Chinese Folk Tale'	104
Explore poetry further	106
Grammar and punctuation	106
Subjects and objects	106
The passive voice	107
Colons	108
Vocabulary and spelling	109
Speaking and listening	110
Have you read?	110
And if you've done all that …	111

Chapter 9 Dealing with disability

Crutches	112
Bones and muscles	114
Your turn to write	115
Improve your writing	116
'Tich Miller'	116
Explore poetry further	118
Grammar and punctuation	118
Pronouns	118
Pronouns in the accusative	121
Inverted commas	122
Vocabulary	122
Spelling	123
Speaking and listening	123
Have you read?	124
And if you've done all that …	124

Chapter 10 Sports

A football story	125
Running all the way to a gold medal	127
Your turn to write	129
Improve your writing	130
'A Subaltern's Love Song'	130
Explore poetry further	133
Grammar and punctuation	133
Agreement of subject and verb	133
Collective nouns	134
Semicolons	136
Vocabulary and spelling	137
To, two and too	138
Speaking and listening	138
Have you read?	139
And if you've done all that …	140

Introduction

The English language

The English language is enormous. It consists of over 500,000 words. Compare that with German which has a vocabulary – or lexicon – of about 185,000 words and French which has fewer than 100,000. Perhaps that's why Shakespeare, the greatest writer, playwright and poet there has ever been anywhere (see Chapter 5) was English. His talents developed partly because of the splendid language he was born into. He couldn't have written in the way that he did in any other language. In fact, you could say that the language produces writers rather than the other way round. Think about that. So why is English so much larger than other European languages? The reasons lie in our history. When the Romans arrived in Britain under Julius Caesar in 55 BC and stayed for over 400 years, they brought Latin. Although most of that disappeared after their final withdrawal in AD 410, we still have a few words in English, such as 'vinegar', which date from the Roman occupation.

The Romans, as you know from your history, also occupied France. There, Latin took a firmer hold than it had done in England. French developed as a language firmly based on Latin – some of which had developed from Ancient Greek. When William of Normandy and his troops invaded England in 1066, they brought the Latin-based French language with them. Gradually that French got mixed with the language which the native Britons were already speaking. Some people call this old, pre-1066 language Anglo-Saxon, but dictionary makers term it Old English or OE.

Words from OE include most of the everyday words we use still such as 'went', 'got', 'ate', 'asked', 'spoke' and many thousands of others. New French words from Latin (or occasionally from Greek) tended to be softer, longer and more elegant.

Old English	Originally from Latin via French
fort	castle
king	sovereign
thought	cogitation
walk	perambulation

So we began to develop a language rich in synonyms (see Chapter 8). We usually have more than one word for things.

By the time Geoffrey Chaucer was writing his famous book *The Canterbury Tales* in the 1390s, Old English had merged fully with French to form a glorious, big, new language which lexicographers – dictionary makers – call Middle English (ME). When Chaucer writes 'He was a verray parfit gentil knight', it isn't too difficult to work out what he means (He was a perfect and very gentle, or genteel, knight).

Fast forward another 200 years to the 1590s and you find Shakespeare writing an early version of modern English – which 21st century readers and listeners can follow quite easily.

Meanwhile, words were flowing into English from all over the world because of our long history as seafarers, travellers, explorers, fighters and conquerors. Wherever English people went, for any reason, their language soaked up local words.

The Crusaders (remember Richard the Lionheart?) went to countries at the east end of the Mediterranean Sea in the Middle Ages to fight for Christianity. Explorers like Walter Raleigh and Francis Drake travelled the world in the 16th century. Nearly two centuries later Captain Cook was sailing round Australia and New Zealand. In Queen Victoria's time David Livingstone and John Speke were the first white men to penetrate parts of Africa.

These are some of the everyday words which have come into English from around the world during the last 1000 years: pyjamas (Persian), parka (Aleutian, an Eskimo or Inuit language), kangaroo (Australian aboriginal), safari (Swahili), wigwam (American Indian), bungalow (Hindi).

The process hasn't stopped, either. Today English is spoken as a first language (in different forms and variations) by about 375 million people across the world. That's more than one fifth of the world population and numbers are growing rapidly because English is the language of the internet.

Meanwhile, back in Britain, about seven per cent of the population is bilingual because they, or their ancestors, moved to Britain from elsewhere. So, words from Caribbean and Indian languages, in particular, are still finding their way into English.

New words are invented to suit new situations, too. A 'nimby' is a 1980s word for someone who doesn't want new building near his or her home. It stood originally for 'Not In My Back Yard'. Computer vocabulary such as 'megabyte' and 'download' are fairly new arrivals too.

So – I hope that point is proved – the English language is colossal, sizeable, huge, gigantic, immense, gargantuan, substantial, massive, tremendous and vast – and we have lots of synonyms!

English is slippery and delicious. It doesn't always work quite as you expect it to. That's what makes it so exciting to work with. It's also what makes it tricky – so it's important to get to grips with as many of the finer points as you can. This book will help you to do so. Each chapter starts with two passages to read. I've selected works by writers whom I admire very much and I hope you will too. Some were written a long time ago. Others are 'hot off the press' and were published only recently.

Both passages are followed by some comprehension questions. These are arranged so that they become progressively more difficult. Some of the final questions are therefore quite challenging, for example, in Exercise 1.1:

6.   Why does Dickens call one basin of gruel 'festive' in the first paragraph (line 4) when in the fifth paragraph he refers to it as a 'meagre meal' (line 25)?

It will help to discuss these questions in class before attempting to write an answer.

Reading will help you to absorb ever more of those half-a-million words which are out there waiting eagerly for you. So, do read as many as you can of the titles listed in the 'Have you read?' sections. Don't be discouraged if you find some of these books are difficult to locate − try searching in your local libraries or in second-hand and specialist booksellers including those found online.

Write as much as you can, too. Writing is to English what running is to sport. It keeps your muscles working and your energy levels high. I am a professional writer as well as a teacher and I know that years of regular writing have done wonders for my command of English. Each chapter has some ideas for you to use as starting points for your own writing.

You will also find in each chapter a poem to study. Each poem is followed by some comprehension questions and some points to spark lively discussion and argument with your classmates.

And don't forget to revise and practise your grammar, spelling and punctuation! Did you know that spelling wasn't fixed until the 18th century and that Shakespeare is said to have spelt his name in thirteen different ways? Don't feel too envious, though. Think how difficult reading must have been when you couldn't tell 'meet' from 'meat' or 'sight' from 'site' or 'lesson' from 'lessen'.

Have fun with it!

Chapter 1 Poor and hungry

The boy who asked for more

Oliver Twist has no family. He lives, in the 1830s, in a workhouse. A workhouse was a building in which paupers (poor people) were kept, often very uncomfortably or even cruelly.

1   The room in which the boys were fed was a large stone hall with a copper[1] at one end. Out of this the master, dressed in an apron for the purpose, and assisted by one or two of the women, ladled the gruel[2] at mealtimes. Of this festive composition each boy had one small portion and no more – except
5   on occasions of great public rejoicing when he had two ounces and a quarter of bread besides.

The bowls never needed washing. The boys polished them with their spoons till they shone. When they had performed this operation (which never took very long, the spoons being nearly as large as the bowls) they
10   would sit eagerly staring at the copper as if they could have devoured the very bricks of which it was composed. They employed themselves meanwhile in sucking their fingers most assiduously with the view of catching any stray splashes of gruel that might have landed there.

Boys generally have excellent appetites. Oliver Twist and his companions
15   had suffered the tortures of slow starvation for three months. At last they got so voracious and wild with hunger that one boy who was tall for his age hinted darkly to his companions that, unless he got another basin of gruel each day, he was afraid he might happen to eat the boy who slept next to him. He had a wild, hungry eye and they believed him.

20   A council was held. The boys drew lots to decide who should walk up to the master that evening and ask for more. The lot fell to Oliver Twist.

The evening arrived and the boys took their places. The master in his cook's uniform stationed himself at the copper. His pauper assistants ranged themselves behind him. The gruel was served out and a long grace was said
25   over the meagre meal.

The gruel disappeared. The boys whispered to each other and winked at Oliver, while his next neighbour nudged him. Child as he was, he was desperate with hunger and reckless with misery. He rose from the table, somewhat alarmed at his own temerity and advancing to the master, basin
30   and spoon in hand, said:

'Please, Sir, I want some more.'

The master was a fat, healthy man but he turned very pale. He gazed in stupefied astonishment at the small rebel for some seconds and then clung for support to the copper. The assistants were paralysed with wonder; the boys with fear.

35

'What?' said the master at length, in a faint voice.

'Please, Sir,' replied Oliver, 'I want some more.'

The master aimed a blow at Oliver's head with the ladle, pinioned him in his arms and shrieked aloud for Mr Bumble, the Beadle.

40

For a week after the commission of the impious and profane offence of asking for more, Oliver Twist remained a close prisoner in a dark and solitary room. It was nice cold weather and he was allowed to wash every morning under the pump in the stone yard in the presence of Mr Bumble, who prevented his catching cold by repeated applications of the cane. And every other day he was carried into the hall where the boys dined and was sociably beaten as a public warning and example.

45

Slightly adapted from *Oliver Twist* by Charles Dickens (1838)

Notes:
[1] A large metal container for heating liquid; this one is built into a brick case
[2] Thin porridge

EXERCISE 1.1

Read the extract from *Oliver Twist* and answer the following questions in complete sentences.

1.   How long was it since the boys had eaten well?

2.   Explain why the bowls never needed washing (line 7).

3.   Why was Oliver the one who asked for more?

4.   How was Oliver punished (a) immediately and (b) during the week after he had asked for more?

5.   Give another word for (a) assiduously (line 12), (b) stationed (line 23), (c) temerity (line 29) and (d) pinioned (line 38).

6.   Why does Dickens call one basin of gruel 'festive' in the first paragraph (line 4) when in the fifth paragraph he refers to it as a 'meagre meal' (line 25)?

World hunger

1   Across the world 1.2 billion people are hungry. These people have too little to eat which means that they are malnourished or do not get enough
5   food to be healthy.

According to a report issued by United Nations Food and Agriculture Organisation in October 2009 this figure is rising. In 2006 about 854
10   million people were undernourished. The 2009 estimate shows a 40% increase in only three years.

There are three reasons for this increase. First, governments and
15   international agencies have not paid enough attention to the farming needs of very poor people. Second, there was a worldwide cash crisis

between 2006 and 2009. Third, food became much more expensive during
20 this time.

1.2 billion people is 15% of the estimated world population of 6.8
billion. Nearly all of the undernourished are in developing countries such as
India and Africa. ? *Not a country*

Children suffer most. Undernourished children suffer up to 160 days of
25 illness each year. Poor nutrition plays a role in nearly half of the 10.9 million
child deaths each year: five million deaths. Under-nutrition worsens the
effect of every disease, including measles and malaria. 70% of malnourished
children live in Asia, 26% in Africa and 4% in Latin America and the
Caribbean.

30 The saddest – and most shocking thing – about all this is that the world
actually produces enough food to feed everyone. If you take all the world's
farming together, and add up what it produces, you find that it generates
17% more calories (or energy units) per person today than it did in 1980.
That means there has been a big increase in food production because world
35 population grew by 70% in the 30 years from 1980 to 2010.

There is enough food in the world to provide everyone in it with at least
2,720 kilocalories (kcal) per person per day. That is plenty for an adult male
and too much for women and children. The problem is that the food is in
the wrong places. Many people in the world do not have sufficient land to
40 grow, or income to purchase, the food they need.

Susan Elkin (2010)

EXERCISE 1.2

Read the extract 'World hunger' and answer the following questions in complete
sentences.

1. What do governments and international agencies need to do to prevent
    people starving?

2. Give two examples of developing areas where many people have too little
    food.

3. How many children die each year because lack of food affects their health?

4. How did the size of the population change in the 30 years to 2010?

5. Roughly how many people in the world have enough to eat? Give (a) a figure in billions and (b) a percentage.

6. How many calories per day is judged as more than enough for a healthy adult male?

7. What, in the author's view, is the worst thing about these facts?

Your turn to write

EXERCISE 1.3

1. Imagine you are Oliver Twist. Write your diary for the day you asked for more and the days which followed. Use your imagination and add to the basic story. Invent as much detail as you like.

2. Write a story about a hungry child in a difficult situation. He or she might be in Britain today or at some point in the past or, perhaps, in some other country where there is hunger today.

3. Do you agree that we could all do more to help starving people? Set out your views in a short article, perhaps for a school magazine or newsletter.

4. Write a detailed description of any television documentary or film you have seen about hunger in a developing country.

5. Write in any way you choose about food, hunger or starvation.

Improve your writing

EXERCISE 1.4

These words can all be used to describe food:

delicious	spicy	sour	sweet	tasty
appetising	unappetising	palatable	toothsome	savoury
unpalatable	bitter	rotten	piquant	mouth-watering
scrumptious	inedible	flavoursome	bland	

Use some of these words to write two short, unrelated paragraphs:

1.   Describe, as accurately as you can, an eating experience which was – for some reason – unpleasant.

2.   Describe an occasion when you enjoyed eating something.

'In the Workhouse'

These four verses are the opening of a 21-verse poem, published in 1879. It is a narrative poem, which means that it tells a story.

1
It is Christmas Day in the Workhouse,
    And the cold bare walls are bright
With garlands of green and holly,
    And the place is a pleasant sight:
5
For with clean-washed hands and faces,
    In a long and hungry line
The paupers sit at the tables,
    For this is the hour they dine.

And the guardians and their ladies,
    Although the wind is east,
10
Have come in their furs and wrappers,
    To watch their charges feast;
To smile and be condescending,
    Put pudding on pauper plates,
15
To be hosts at the workhouse banquet
    They've paid for with their rates.

Oh, the paupers are meek and lowly
    With their 'Thank'ee kindly mum's';
So long as they fill their stomachs,
20
    What matter whence it comes?
But one of the old men mutters,
    And pushes his plate aside:
'Great God!' he cries 'But it chokes me!
    For this is the day she died.'

25   The guardians gazed in horror,
            The master's face went white;
      'Did a pauper refuse his pudding?'
            Could their ears believe aright?
      Then the ladies clutched their husbands,
30   Thinking the man would die,
      Struck by a bolt, or something,
            By the outraged one on high.

George R Sims (1879)

EXERCISE 1.5

Read 'In the Workhouse' and answer the following questions in complete sentences.

1. What is being given to the paupers?

2. In line 4 the workhouse is described as 'a pleasant sight'. Which of the people mentioned in the poem, if any, would describe it so positively?

3. How does the clothing of the visitors differ from that worn by the workhouse residents?

4. What does one of the old men do which surprises everyone?

5. Who is 'the outraged one on high'?

6. What do you learn about the attitude of the visitors from the words 'pleasant', 'condescending' and 'banquet'?

 Discuss

EXERCISE 1.6

1. How do you think the story might develop?

2. Sims was a journalist who believed very strongly in social justice. Are there any signs of this in the poem?

3. *Oliver Twist* was published in 1838. Do you think George Sims had read it? In what ways is 'In The Workhouse' similar to the extract from *Oliver Twist*? In what ways is 'In the Workhouse' different from *Oliver Twist*?

   Think about: ● characters ● story ● the way the story is told.

4. 'In the Workhouse' consists of 21 eight-line verses. Each has the same pattern of rhyme, starting or ending on alternate lines as follows:

   What does this careful pattern add or take away from the poem?

   A
   (B)
   C
   (B)
   D
   (E)
   F
   (E)

✴ Explore poetry further

Find the rest of the poem – in an anthology or on the internet – and read it in full. Work out whether you think it achieves what George Sims wanted to do. How effective do you find it as a poem?

Grammar and punctuation

Full stops

Every sentence must end in a full stop. Sometimes the full stop is part of a question mark or an exclamation mark. You might see

> **. ?** or **!**

at the end of sentences. It is quite wrong to end a sentence in any other way – for example with a comma.

Use a question mark if your sentence asks a question such as:

- Is that child hungry?

Use an exclamation mark if your sentence says something unexpected or makes a surprised comment such as:

- That child is hungry!

Use a full stop for all other sorts of sentence, such as:

- No child should be hungry.

We shall review the use of question marks and exclamation marks later. In this chapter we concentrate on the full stop.

Starting a sentence

Make sure you start the first word of a new sentence with a capital letter. You should also make the difference between capital and small letters very clear.

Sometimes capital letters are called 'upper case' letters. Similarly small letters are sometimes known as 'lower case' letters. This is because printers used to store their individual letters in separate containers (cases) one above the other. The upper case contained the capital letters and the lower one the small letters. Old-fashioned typewriters copied this arrangement.

Capital/upper case:

> **A B C D E F G H I J K L M N O P Q R S T U V W X Y Z**

Small/lower case:

> **a b c d e f g h i j k l m n o p q r s t u v w x y z**

EXERCISE 1.7

Write out the sentences below with the capital letters and full stops in the right places. Each one consists of two sentences.

1. life in a Victorian workhouse was very harsh residents were often hungry

2. at times Oliver felt very lonely his mother had died when he was born

3. many children in Africa are starving more could be done to help

4. vegetables are good for you too many burgers are not

5. Oliver asked the other boys watched

6. some people in Britain choose to eat too much many African children do not have that choice

EXERCISE 1.8

Five of these are complete sentences. The other three are not. Write out the ones which are already sentences with a capital letter at the beginning and a full stop at the end. Ignore the others.

1. *Oliver Twist* and *Nicholas Nickleby*, books by Charles Dickens

2. Dickens wrote *Oliver Twist*

3. Some people are starving

4. oranges are my favourite fruit

5. you should always eat your greens

6. spinach and broccoli

7. yams are a basic food in Africa

8. the Chinese restaurant near us

Now add words of your own to convert the three you have left over into correctly punctuated sentences.

EXERCISE 1.9

1. Write out this story with capital letters and full stops in the right places:

   Emma has had a bad week on Monday she was late for school because of a traffic jam Tuesday was worse there was rice for lunch Emma hates rice on Wednesday she cut her finger on the bread knife at breakfast time things got worse as the week went on in the supermarket with her mother on Thursday Emma dropped a dozen eggs as she was putting them in the trolley then on Friday she fell over the cat and sprained her ankle so she went to bed early on Friday evening she had a nightmare

2. If you get that finished quickly, write a few lines of your own in which everything goes right for Emma. Make sure every sentence begins with a capital letter and ends with a full stop.

Nouns

A noun is the name given to a person, place or thing. There are three main types of noun: common, proper and abstract.

(a) The following words are all **common** nouns:

   gruel   spoons

   man   pauper

   children   fruit

(b) Names of people, for example Charles Dickens, Mr Bumble or Susan Elkin, are **proper** nouns. So are the names of towns such as Horsham or of rivers such as the Tyne or the Thames. Proper nouns *always* begin with a capital letter.

(c) Finally, **abstract** nouns are nouns which name feelings, ideas or things which we talk and write about but which can't be touched:

   diet   problems

   starvation   hunger

   improvement   misery

EXERCISE 1.10

Noun activities:

1.   Think of a fruit or vegetable for every letter of the alphabet. Have fun with this and try to think of some unusual ones: avocado, breadfruit, chard, damson … These are ordinary, **common** nouns.

2.   Think of a boy's name, which is a **proper** noun, for every letter of the alphabet. Be as unusual as you can. Augustus, Bartholomew, Cuthbert … If you write them down, check that you have used a capital letter for the first letter of each name. Then repeat the exercise with girls' names. You are working, remember, with proper nouns.

3.   Write down the word for every feeling you can think of, such as sadness, hunger, joy, excitement, thirst, tiredness … These are **abstract** nouns.

Vocabulary and spelling

1.   **Voracious** means hungry. It is related to the word **devour** which means 'to swallow' or 'eat up greedily'. The following words also often mean 'hungry' although they can be used in slightly different senses:

    gluttonous   ravenous   ravening   craving   greedy   rapacious

Look up the exact meaning of these words in a dictionary and experiment with them in sentences of your own.

2.   **Crucial** means 'central'. It comes from the Latin word for 'cross' (*crux*, *crucis*). If something is crucial it is as if it is at the centre of a cross and therefore very important.

If you say something is 'the **crux** of the matter' you mean it is the centre point of the issue.

Jesus was **crucified** or attached to a cross to die.
Cruciform or **cruciate** means 'shaped like a cross'.
A **cruciverbalist** is someone who loves crosswords.
Use these words in sentences of your own.

3. Look at the spelling of **meagre**. It ends with '-re'. So do:

theatre   centre   acre   ochre   sabre

Do not muddle these with similar sounding words which end in '-er' and do not be confused if you see these words spelt otherwise. Americans have different spelling rules so you have to be on your guard if you are using British English; and beware the spellcheck on your computer – it is often set to American spellings!

4. **Immediate** has a double 'm'. So do:

command	common	commit	grammar
glimmer	hammer	commence	hammock
immense	recommend	accommodate	commerce
clammy	commission	ammonia	commotion

Learn the spellings of these words by writing them down several times. Look up the meanings of any that you do not know.

Speaking and listening

1. Write a class play out of the incident in *Oliver Twist* when Oliver asks for more. Perhaps you could perform it to the rest of the school in assembly.

2. Work with a partner. Choose a charity which works with the poor in developing countries. Prepare a talk for the rest of the class about it.

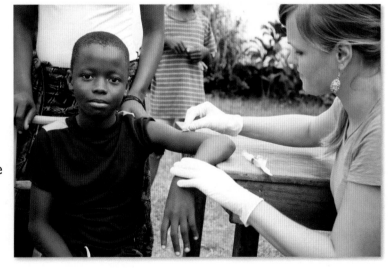

3. Work with someone in the class you don't know very well. Find out what he or she likes to eat. Take it in turns to do this. Then join with another pair. Tell the other pair about your partner's eating preferences and dislikes.

4. Get a copy of *Oliver Twist* – or any other book by Charles Dickens. Find a short passage that appeals to you and practise reading it aloud. Then hear each other's readings in small groups.

Have you read?

All these books are about children who are hungry or poor or both:

- *Oliver Twist* by Charles Dickens (1838)
- *A Christmas Carol* by Charles Dickens (1843)
- *Black Harvest* by Ann Pilling (1983)
- *Rice Without Rain* by Minfong Ho (1986)
- *The Breadwinner* by Deborah Ellis (2000)
- *The Family From One End Street* by Eve Garnett (1937)
- *Garbage King* by Elizabeth Laird (2003)

✔ And if you've done all that ...

- Find out about the life of Charles Dickens through encyclopaedias and the internet. Prepare a short talk about him for the rest of the class.

- Do some research into Victorian recipes. Do we have comparable recipes today? Make a class recipe leaflet or booklet that includes both Victorian and modern-day recipes or, alternatively, collect from each pupil in your class a favourite family recipe. If you can use a computer to make the booklet look professional, you might be able to sell it to parents and friends in aid of one of the charities working with hungry children, such as Save the Children (www.savethechildren.org.uk) or Oxfam (www.oxfam.org.uk).

- Read *Oliver Twist*. Then watch the 1968 film of Lionel Bart's musical *Oliver!* and/or the 2005 film *Oliver Twist* directed by Roman Polanski. If your school does not have a DVD of these, you will be able to borrow them from almost any library. In which ways are the stories different? Why do you think the film makers made these changes?

Chapter 2 In the water

Saved from drowning

Roger and Polly are rowing with their mysterious French friend
Melusine on a canal at La Venise Verte in the Vendée area of France.

1   'We can't change places here. I'll pull into the bank.' Roger laid hold of the
       oars and prepared to turn.

       'It's okay. I'll just –'

       Polly stood up just as he started to turn toward the bank – hit her head on
5   the half-fallen tree – and fell straight out of the boat.

       The clonk of her head hitting the wood, the leap of the boat as she left it
       and the loud splash caused Roger to drop the oars and spin round. She
       hadn't screamed. She vanished into the scummy water and it closed over
       her head without sound.

10   'Polly! Polly!' he bellowed, more in fury than in fright at first. Then, when
       nothing happened, his voice rose to a squeak of terror. '*Polly!*'

       Silence. Roger's wits completely deserted him. He half stood, half crouched
       there in the rocking boat, expecting her head to break the surface,
       expecting – expecting it not to have happened.

15   But it had. She was gone.

       Suddenly the boat leapt again. Instinctively he clutched the gunwales to
       steady himself, and looked toward the stern.

       Melusine was gone.

       He saw only the swirl in the green water beside where she had been
20   seated. And something – a blackish undulating line – her pigtail? – wiggled,
       swished audibly through the turbulence and disappeared.

       Desperately he prepared to jump in. But something stopped him. There was
       some underwater upheaval occurring just below the boat that upset his
       balance and made him crouch down again instinctively. Something big was
25   threshing about down there.

       Roger was paralysed with shock, with fear. He could think of only one thing,
       sitting there clinging to the oarlocks with white knuckles.

       A crocodile … impossible! And yet …

30 Then suddenly there was a bubbling burst of sound. Polly's head had shot out of the water as if propelled from below. Her face was ghastly, deathly white under streaks of glistening mud, her hair

35 plastered to her skull.

As Roger reached out and grabbed any bit of her he could get hold of he felt her body being

40 shoved higher by something unseen in the depths.

Polly lay in the bottom of the boat, streams of water pouring

45 from her hair, her clothes. He threw himself onto her back with all his strength and more water gushed out of her mouth and nose. She gave a retching cough and then he heard a great noisy gasp of air rush into her lungs. It was the most marvellous relieving

50 sound he had ever heard in his life.

Melusine …!

He looked round wildly. And at once he saw her! He felt all the blood leave his face.

She was crouching in the boat just behind him. Her face was pale, exhausted

55 even, but composed. After drying Polly a little, she took off her life jacket and after it the jacket she was wearing. She spread this lengthways over Polly to warm her.

Roger crouched there, unable to move. His eyes were riveted to the jacket.

It was perfectly dry.

60 Roger reached out and touched the leg of Melusine's trousers.

They were dry. *She was dry all over.* Her pigtail, that he had distinctly seen vanishing into the canal, was dry. She had not a drop of water on her.

Slightly abridged from *Melusine* by Lynne Reid Banks (1988)

EXERCISE 2.1

Read the extract 'Melusine' and answer the following questions in complete sentences.

1. Explain how Polly comes to fall out of the boat.

2. Give another word for (a) turbulence (line 21), (b) propelled (line 31) and (c) riveted (line 58).

3. Why does Roger not jump into the water to rescue Polly?

4. What indications are there in this passage that Melusine is not quite what she seems?

5. List six words from the passage which suggest Roger's fear.

6. Why do you think Lynne Reid Banks often uses very short sentences and paragraphs in this extract?

A mermaid-like sea mammal

1   The dugong, or sea cow, lives in the south-west Pacific and the Indian Ocean.

A sea cow's life is not a demanding one. They trundle through the underwater meadows
5   propelled entirely by the slow downward sweep of their huge tail. Since they live on plants, and plants need light in order to grow, they have no reason to swim to any depth. They are so big that few other swimmers can
10   attack them and sharks only seldom venture into these shallow waters.

Dugongs live off the tropical coasts of Australia in scattered herds and tend to patrol the same paths like a herd of domestic terrestrial cows.

When a young sea cow is born it suckles milk from a nipple in its mother's armpit. Since it and its mother are, of course, air-breathing the mothers may
15   at this time rear out of the water to allow their drinking young to breathe. It is this, some say, that gave rise to legends of the mermaid.

Slightly adapted from *The Life of Mammals* by David Attenborough (2002)

EXERCISE 2.2

Read the extract 'A mermaid-like sea mammal' and answer the following questions in complete sentences.

1. In what three ways is the dugong's life 'not a demanding one'?

2. Where are sea cows found? Be as accurate as you can.

3. Which is the only animal which might attack a dugong?

4. Why is the sea cow associated with mermaids?

5. Which two words suggest that David Attenborough does not fully believe that the sea cow could be mistaken for a mermaid?

Your turn to write

EXERCISE 2.3

1. Write a story about a mermaid (or merman).

2. Describe a sea mammal in careful detail. You might choose a seal, dolphin, whale or sea lion, for example. Include its appearance, habits, where it lives, its food, breeding and so on. Use reference books or the internet to find the information and your own knowledge if you have seen the creature yourself or watched a TV programme about it.

3. Read one of the books listed in 'Have you read?' on page 31. Write a review of it.

4. Write about water in any way you choose.

5. Imagine you are Roger in the extract from *Melusine*. Write a letter or an email to a friend at home in England describing what happened at the canal. Invent as much extra detail of your own as you like.

✎ Improve your writing

EXERCISE 2.4

Finish these sentences as interestingly as you can:

1. Although I have never seen a mermaid …

2. Mermaids …

3. In the sea …

4. Like all sea creatures …

5. Dugongs …

6. Many stories about mermaids …

'The Mermaid'

Alfred Tennyson wrote this poem in 1830 when he was only 21 years old.

```
        I.
1       Who would be
        A mermaid fair,
        Singing alone,
        Combing her hair
5       Under the sea,
        In a golden curl
        With a comb of pearl,

        II.
        I would be a mermaid fair;
        I would sing to myself the whole of the day;
10      With a comb of pearl I would comb my hair;
        And still as I comb'd I would sing and say,
        Who is it loves me? Who loves not me?
        I would comb my hair till my ringlets would fall
        Low adown, low adown,
15      From under my starry sea-bud crown
        Low adown and around,
        And I should look like a fountain of gold
```

Springing alone
With a shrill inner sound,
20 Over the throne
In the midst of the hall;
Till that great sea-snake under the sea
From his coiled sleeps in the central deeps
Would slowly trail himself sevenfold
25 Round the hall where I sate, and look in at the gate
With his large calm eyes for the love of me.
And all the mermen under the sea
Would feel their immortality
Die in their hearts for the love of me.

III.
30 But at night I would wander away, away,
I would fling on each side my low-flowing locks,
And lightly vault from the throne and play
With the mermen in and out of the rocks;
We would run to and fro, and hide and seek,
35 On the broad sea-wolds in the crimson shells,
Whose silvery spikes are nighest the sea.
But if any came near I would call, and shriek,
And adown the steep like a wave I would leap
From the diamond-ledges that jut from the dells;
40 For I would not be kiss'd by all who would list,
Of the bold merry mermen under the sea;
They would sue me, and woo me, and flatter me,
In the purple twilights under the sea;
But the king of them all would carry me,
45 Woo me, and win me, and marry me,
In the branching jaspers under the sea;
Then all the dry pied things that be
In the hueless mosses under the sea
Would curl round my silver feet silently,
50 All looking up for the love of me.
And if I should carol aloud, from aloft
All things that are forked, and horned, and soft
Would lean out from the hollow sphere of the sea,
All looking down for the love of me.

Alfred, Lord Tennyson (1830)

EXERCISE 2.5

Write the answers to these questions using complete sentences:

1. What colour is the mermaid's hair?

2. What does she like to do during the day?

3. What creatures love her?

4. Explain the meaning of (a) immortality (line 28), (b) vault (line 32), (c) jaspers (line 46) and (d) hueless (line 48).

5. What does the mermaid like to do at night?

 Discuss

EXERCISE 2.6

1. How do the poem's three sections differ from one another? Why do you think the poet chose to arrange it in this way?

2. Would you describe this poem as:
   - a dream
   - a fantasy
   - a story
   - an idea

   something else and, if so, what?

3. Why do you think the poet uses the word 'me' so many times. What effect does this have on the tone of the poem?

4. Some people say that Tennyson is a musical poet. Are there any ways in which 'The Mermaid' is a musical poem?

 Explore poetry further

Find out as much as you can about the life and work of Lord Tennyson. Design a set of PowerPoint slides about him and use them as the basis of a presentation for the rest of the class.

Grammar and punctuation

Question marks

The question mark is very easy. Whenever the writer or a character in a story asks a question, it is followed by a question mark instead of a full stop. Most questions ask how, who, what, where, when or why.

For example:

- When did you read a book by Lynne Reid Banks?
- Why doesn't David Attenborough believe in mermaids?
- 'Was it Melusine's pigtail?' wondered Roger.

EXERCISE 2.7

Some of these sentences are, or include, questions. Others are not or do not. Write out the ones which need question marks. (You should have five.)

1. Why wasn't Melusine wet

2. Melusine was dry

3. Fortunately Polly did not drown

4. What do dugongs eat

5. Does the dugong have another name

6. How many books has David Attenborough written

7. In 2002 he wrote *Life on Air*

8. Roger said 'I simply can't believe it'

9. 'Who got me out of the canal' asked Polly

A spoken question mark

In speech, British speakers of English usually lift the pitch of their voices (like singing a higher note) at the end of questions. It is a sort of spoken question mark.

Australian speakers of English do this with almost every sentence. Because we are so used to hearing Australian speech on TV, many British speakers of English (particularly young people) are beginning to do this too. It has the rather funny (to old-fashioned British ears) effect of making everything sound like a question.

Traditionally we drop the pitch of our voices (lower note) at the end of a statement – a spoken full stop. Experiment with saying:

'Sea cows are mammals'

and

'Sea cows are mammals ...?'

Say it first as a firm statement. Listen to where your voice goes. Now say it as a question and as if you are tentative or not sure of the answer. Your voice will have gone up.

EXERCISE 2.8

Make as many words of four letters and more as you can out of:

QUESTION MARK

Verbs

Verbs are the most important words in any language. They are 'action words' or 'being words'. They tell us what nouns are 'doing' or what they 'are'. Verbs are the glue which holds sentences together. If a group of words has no verb then it isn't really a sentence.

These are verbs:

bellowed	clutched	swished	wiggled	prepared
shoved	grabbed	gushed	trundle	suckles

Verbs such as those above often end in '-s' or '-ed' depending on who is performing the action and when. They often consist of two or more words. The extra words which 'help' the main verb are usually parts of the verbs 'to be' or 'to have' and are known as 'auxiliary' verbs. For example:

Present: is going

Future: will go, will have gone, will be gone

Past: was going, had gone, had been going

These words are used to change the tense of the verb, in other words to say when the action of the verb occurs (past, present or future). Good writers always choose strong colourful verbs.

EXERCISE 2.9

Put verbs of your own in the gaps in the following sentences:

1. Water _____ from the roof.

2. Roger _____ himself free.

3. We _____ France.

4. My father _____ the kettle and _____ the tea.

5. Dugongs _____ in the sea.

6. David Attenborough often _____ on television.

7. Tomorrow I shall _____.

EXERCISE 2.10

Write out the following passage and underline the verbs. The first three have been done for you.

It <u>was</u> evening. Polly <u>had been seen</u> by a local doctor who <u>had wanted</u> to take her to hospital in Niort, the nearest large town 30 miles away, but in the end he had agreed that her mother could nurse her at home. He'd bandaged the bump on her head and said that she'd had a very narrow escape from drowning. When he said this, he scowled at her parents in a way that made them both hang their heads like guilty children.

Vocabulary and spelling

1. **Audibly** means something is said or done so that it can be heard. It comes from the Latin verb *audio* which means 'I hear'.

   An **audience** was originally a group of people who listen to words or music. The word is now used more loosely to include people who watch something or even read it.

   Audio-visual equipment is something like a DVD player which allows the user to hear as well as see.

   The nerve which goes to the brain from the back of the ear is the **auditory** nerve.

An **auditorium** is the space in a theatre where the **audience** sits.

Audiology is the scientific study of hearing.

Audio-description is a system of explaining visual effects in a play or other performance for blind people.

2. **Terrestrial** means 'of the earth' (rather than of the sea or the air). It comes from the Latin word *terra* which means 'earth' or 'land'.

Angleterre, as the French call England, means 'land of the Angles'. (Remember your Anglo-Saxons?)

Your **territory** is the land you are familiar with, own or have a right to.

Traditional reddish garden flower pots are made of **terracotta** (baked earth).

An **extra-terrestrial** being comes from another world (particularly in films and stories).

3. Check that you know these ten spellings. All the words come from the two passages at the beginning of this chapter.

straight	deserted	instinctively	something	disappeared
desperately	relieving	exhausted	domestic	breathing

4. **They're, their, there**

They're means they are. The apostrophe marks the place of the missing letter. So 'They're hungry' means 'They are hungry' and 'They're arguing' means 'They are arguing'.

Their is a possessive pronoun (see Chapter 9). It means 'belonging to them'. Melusine was the friend belonging to Roger and Polly so she was **their** friend. Dugongs find the food which belongs to them in shallow waters. They find **their** food.

If you mean anything other than 'they are' or 'belonging to them', use **there**.

Words such as these which **sound** the same but which have different spellings and meanings are called **homophones**.

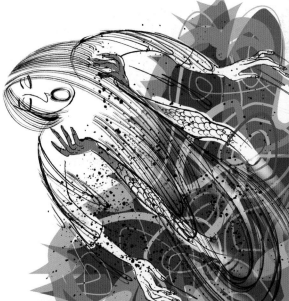

EXERCISE 2.11

Write **they're**, **their** or **there** in the spaces in these sentences:

1. Dogs wag _____ tails when _____ happy.

2. Roger will moor the boat over _____.

3. _____ are some sea cows suckling _____ young.

4. Polly and Melusine were both in the water so Roger, _____ companion, was frightened.

5. Some mammals live _____ lives in water.

6. The trees over _____ will shed _____ leaves soon because _____ not evergreen.

7. Once upon a time _____ was a poor woodcutter.

8. _____ reading 'The Kraken' by Alfred Lord Tennyson in _____ English lesson today.

9. Sir David Attenborough's books and TV programmes have taught millions of people more about _____ world.

10. In our class the boys tend to like _____ space while the girls enjoy _____ close chats.

Speaking and listening

1. Work with a partner. One of you pretends to believe in mermaids, the other does not. Rehearse your argument until it is like a little play. Then perform it to the rest of the class. You could also record it as a podcast.

2. Work in a group. Pretend you are making a television advertisement for a trip to Australia to see the sea cows. You have to find ways of making it sound really attractive so that anyone seeing the advertisement will want to pay to go on the trip.

3. Work in a group of three. Take the parts of Roger, Polly and Melusine. Act out what happened in the boat. Use your own words and add extra details of your own.

4. Read one of the books on the list below. Then tell the rest of the class what you liked or disliked about it. If you enjoyed it, work out what you can say to persuade others to read it.

5. Describe to a partner in as much detail as you can your earliest memory of going in, or on, some kind of boat.

Have you read?

Most of these books are about children in boats or about mermaids:

- *Melusine* by Lynne Reid Banks (1988)
- *The Life of Mammals* by David Attenborough (2002)
- *The Little Mermaid* retold by Andrew Matthews (2000)
- *The Dolphin Crossing* by Jill Paton Walsh (1967)
- *Black Ivory* by Norman Collins (1948)
- *In Deep Water* by Michelle Magorian (1992)
- *The Great Elephant Chase* by Gillian Cross (1992)
- *Swallows and Amazons* by Arthur Ransome (1930)
- *Nation* by Terry Pratchett (2008)
- *Anila's Journey* by Mary Finn (2008)
- *Journey to the River Sea* by Eva Ibbotson (2001)
- *The Adventures of Huckleberry Finn* by Mark Twain (1884)

And if you've done all that ...

- Research the legend of Melusine via the internet or in an encyclopaedia. The German composer Felix Mendelssohn (1809–47) wrote a piece of music called *The Fair Melusine*. Find it and listen to it. Your school music department may be able to help you find it or you could consult BBC Radio 3 which specialises in classical music (www.bbc.co.uk/radio3). Decide how well you think the music fits the legend.

- Read two of the books on the list above and compare them in a written review. Say how they are different and what they have in common. Which did you prefer and why?

Chapter 3 Animals

The Elephant's Child

1 Once, a very long time ago, the elephant had no trunk. All he had was a blackish, bulgy nose as big as a boot. He could wriggle it about from side to side but he couldn't pick things up with it.

Then a new elephant – an elephant's child – was born in Africa. He was full
5 of 'satiable curtiosity' which means he asked a lot of questions, although he was always very polite.

He asked his tall aunt the Ostrich why her tail feathers grew just so. He asked his tall uncle the Giraffe what made his skin spotty. He asked his broad aunt the Hippopotamus why her eyes were red and he asked his
10 hairy uncle the Baboon why melons tasted just so. They all told him off and shouted at him crossly, but he went on asking questions about everything he saw, heard, felt, smelt or touched because he was still full of 'satiable curtiosity'.

One fine morning this 'satiable elephant's child' asked a fine new question,
15 most politely: 'What does the crocodile have for dinner?'

His aunts and uncles all answered 'Hush!' in a loud and dreadful tone. They all looked very angry with him. Suddenly the elephant's child saw the kolokolo bird perched on a thorn bush.

'Everyone is cross with me because of my "satiable curtiosity,"' he told the
20 kolokolo bird, 'but I still want to know what the crocodile has for dinner.'

The kolokolo bird replied with a mournful cry, 'Go to the banks of the great, grey-green, greasy Limpopo River all set about with fever trees and find out.'

So, next morning the elephant's child assembled a hundred pounds of
25 bananas (the short, red kind), a hundred pounds of sugar cane (the long, purple kind) and seventeen melons (the green, crinkly kind). He said goodbye to his grumpy family. Then he set off on a long journey. As he went, he looked about him, he munched melons, he ate bananas and he crunched sugar cane. He threw down the rind, skins and leaves because, remember,
30 he had no trunk with which to pick up his litter.

At last he came to the banks of the great, grey-green, greasy Limpopo River all set about with fever trees, just as the kolokolo bird had said. Now, of course, until that very week and day and hour, the elephant's child had never seen a crocodile. It was all his 'satiable curtiosity'.

35   The first thing the elephant's child found at the great, grey-green, greasy Limpopo River all set about with fever trees was a bi-coloured python rock snake. It was curled round a rock and had a scalesome, flailsome tail. ''Scuse me,' said the elephant's child, 'but have you seen a crocodile in these provocative parts, and if you have, could you tell me what he has for
40   dinner?'

Like the elephant's child's aunts and uncles back home, the bi-coloured python rock snake crossly refused to answer. So the elephant's child walked along the bank of the great, grey-green, greasy Limpopo River scattering melon rinds he couldn't pick up – until he trod on what he thought was a
45   log. But really it was a crocodile! The crocodile winked cunningly and shed a few crocodile tears.

''Scuse me,' said the elephant's child most politely, 'but do you happen to have seen a crocodile in these provocative parts? And, if you have, could you tell me what he has for dinner, please?' The crocodile winked the other
50   eye and lifted his tail out of the mud.

'Come hither little one,' said the crocodile. 'Why do you ask such things?'

'My tall aunt the Ostrich, my tall uncle the Giraffe, my broad aunt the Hippopotamus, my hairy uncle the Baboon and the bi-coloured python rock snake all got furious with me when I asked but I still want to know,' said the
55   elephant's child.

'Come hither little one,' said the crocodile, 'for I am the crocodile. Come hither and I'll whisper.' Then the elephant's child put his head down close to the crocodile's musky, tusky mouth and the crocodile caught him by his little nose which, until that moment, had been no bigger than a boot,
60   although much more useful.

'I think,' said the crocodile, through his teeth, 'that today I will begin with this elephant's child.'

The elephant's child was frightened and tried to back away, shouting through his nose: 'Led go! You're hurdig me!'

65   Then the bi-coloured python rock snake scuffled down the bank and said: 'My young friend, tug as hard as ever you can or that crocodile will quickly jerk you into yonder limpid stream.' (This is the way bi-coloured python rock snakes always talk.)

70 So the elephant's child sat back on his little haunches and pulled and pulled and pulled until his nose began to stretch. The crocodile flailed about in the water making it all creamy with great sweeps of his tail. He too pulled and pulled and pulled.

The elephant's child's nose grew longer and longer. He stretched all four of his little legs and pulled and pulled and pulled. The crocodile threshed his
75 tail like an oar as he pulled and pulled and pulled. By now the elephant's child's nose was hurting a lot and was nearly five feet long. 'This is too butch for me,' he said through his long nose.

Then the bi-coloured python rock snake came down the bank and knotted his scalesome, flailsome tail tightly round the elephant's child's hind legs. He
80 pulled and the elephant's child pulled and the crocodile pulled but the bi-coloured python rock snake pulled the hardest. At last the crocodile let go of the elephant's child with a plop you could hear all up and down the Limpopo (still great, grey-green, greasy and all set about with fever trees).

The elephant's child carefully put wet banana leaves on his sore nose and
85 sat on the bank of the great, grey-green, greasy Limpopo river for three days waiting for his stretched nose to shrink. But the bi-coloured python rock snake told him it wouldn't grow any shorter and it didn't. The crocodile had pulled it into a really-truly trunk, the same as all elephants have today.

90   After a while a fly came and stung him on the shoulder. Before he knew what he was doing the elephant's child had lifted up his trunk and hit that fly dead with the end of it.

"Vantage number one!' said the bi-coloured python rock snake. 'You couldn't have done that with a mere-smear nose. Try and eat a little now.'

95   Before he could think what he was doing the elephant's child had put out his trunk, plucked a large bundle of grass, dusted it clean against his fore legs and stuffed it into his own mouth.

"Vantage number two!' said the bi-coloured python rock snake. 'You couldn't have done that with a mere-smear nose. Don't you think the sun is

100   awfully hot here?'

'It is,' said the elephant's child and, before he had thought about it, he had schlooped up a schloop of mud from the banks of the great, grey-green, greasy Limpopo River and slapped it on his head where it made a cool schloopy-sloshy mud-cap all trickly behind his ears.

105   "Vantage number three!' said the bi-coloured python rock snake. 'You couldn't have done that with a mere-smear nose.'

With that the elephant's child thanked the bi-coloured python rock snake, said goodbye and set off on the long journey home across Africa to his family. As he went he frisked and whisked his new trunk.

110   When he wanted grass he could pick it up from the ground without bending. When flies bit him he used his trunk to break off a branch of a tree to use as a fly-swat. When he felt hot in the African sun his trunk made him a slushy-squashy mud-cap.

If he felt lonely he sang to himself through his trunk and made a trumpeting

115   noise louder than several brass bands. As he went along he picked up the melon rinds, banana skins and sugar-cane leaves he had dropped on his way there, for he was a tidy pachyderm.

At last he reached home. There, several members of his family spoke to him: his brothers, his hairy uncle the Baboon, his tall aunt the Ostrich, his tall

120   uncle the Giraffe and his broad aunt the Hippopotamus. 'Oh bananas! What have you done to your nose?' asked one of his brothers.

'I got a new one from the crocodile on the banks of the great, grey-green, greasy Limpopo River,' explained the elephant's child. 'I asked him what he had for dinner and he gave me this to keep.'

125   'It looks very ugly,' said his hairy uncle the Baboon, cross as usual.

'It does, but it's useful,' replied the elephant's child, using his trunk to pick up his hairy uncle the Baboon and throw him into a wasps' nest.

Then that bad elephant's child took his revenge on all his relations who had been so bad-tempered with him in the past. This is what he did: he pulled
130   out his tall Ostrich aunt's tail feathers. He caught his tall uncle the Giraffe by the hind-legs and dragged him through a thorn bush and he shouted at his broad aunt the Hippopotamus and blew bubbles into her ear when she was sleeping in the water after meals. But he never let anyone touch the kolokolo bird.

135   At last things grew so exciting that all his family went off one by one in a hurry to the banks of the great, grey-green, greasy Limpopo River all set about with fever trees, to borrow new noses from the crocodile. That is why all the elephants you will ever see, beside all those that you won't, have trunks like that of the 'satiably curtious' elephant's child.

Slightly adapted by Susan Elkin from *Just So Stories*
by Rudyard Kipling (1902)

EXERCISE 3.1

Read 'The Elephant's Child' and answer the following questions in complete sentences.

1. Why did the elephant's child leave his family?

2. Apart from the elephant's child, which animal do you find the most interesting in this story? Explain your choice.

3. Give another word for (a) assembled (line 24), (b) hither (line 61) and (c) threshed (line 74).

4. Explain why the elephant's child is pleased with his new trunk.

5. When the elephant's child uses the words 'satiable curtiosity' (e.g. in line 12) and 'provocative' (e.g. in line 39) he is making mistakes in his English because he is still very young. Can you work out what he really means?

Elephants in zoos

1   Sir,

The RSPCA[1] wants zoos to stop keeping elephants because of animal welfare concerns. It has nothing to do with politics, as suggested by Richard Morrison (T2, September 29). RSPCA-commissioned scientific research
5   shows that elephants in European zoos live nowhere near the 60–65 years they can reach in the wild. They die young, having suffered from deficient enclosures, poor diet, illness, inappropriate social grouping and even rough treatment by their handlers. Zoo-breeding programmes also have an abysmal record – about a third of zoo-born babies die within a year, many
10   of which are stillborn, or rejected or even killed by their mothers.

Because they fail to keep flourishing captive populations, zoos have to import elephants from their native lands. Yet they claim to keep elephants for conservation reasons. The costs of housing elephants properly in European zoos are prohibitive, and that money would be better spent
15   protecting elephants in the wild.

Yours sincerely,
ROB ATKINSON
(Head, Wildlife Department),
RSPCA, Southwater, Horsham,
20   West Sussex RH13 9RS
October 3rd
Published in *The Times* (October 2003)

Note:[1] The Royal Society for the Prevention of Cruelty to Animals

EXERCISE 3.2

Read the letter about elephants in zoos and answer the following questions in complete sentences.

1.   What is Rob Atkinson's job?

2.   Where is the RSPCA's head office?

3.   Why does Mr Atkinson think it is cruel to keep elephants in zoos?

4.   What would Mr Atkinson prefer the money for housing the elephants be spent on?

5.   What has made Mr Atkinson write this letter to *The Times* newspaper?

6.   Give another word for (a) deficient (line 6), (b) abysmal (line 9) and (c) prohibitive (line 14).

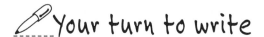 Your turn to write

EXERCISE 3.3

1.   Write your own *Just So* story of how the dog got its bark, how the tiger got its stripes, how the bird got its wings or how the kangaroo got its pocket.

2.   Imagine you are an elephant and tell the story of something which has happened to you. You could set your story in Africa or India or in a zoo.

3.   What do you think about elephants in zoos? Do some research on the subject and then write a letter to *The Times* either agreeing or disagreeing with Mr Atkinson.

4.   Did you enjoy 'The Elephant's Child'? Write your views. Say what you liked and disliked about it.

5.   Imagine that you are trying to communicate with someone who has never seen, heard, touched or smelled an elephant. He or she has never even seen a picture in a book or on television. Describe an elephant for him or her to give a clear sense of the animal. Don't forget to mention its appearance, size, colour, shape, habits, the sounds it makes and how it smells.

'Two Performing Elephants'

This poem was published in 1929 when it was usual for circuses to feature trained, performing animals.

1   He stands with his forefeet on the drum
    and the other, the old one, the pallid hoary female
    must creep her great bulk under the bridge of him.

    On her knees, in utmost caution
5   all agog, and curling up her trunk
    she edges through without upsetting him.
    Triumph! The ancient pig-tailed monster!

    When her trick is to climb over him
    with what shadow-like slow carefulness
10   she skims him, sensitive
    as shadows from ages gone and perished
    in touching him, and planting her round feet.

    While the wispy modern children, half afraid
    watch silent. The looming of the hoary, far-gone ages
15   is too much for them.

    DH Lawrence (1929)

EXERCISE 3.4

Read 'Two Performing Elephants' and answer the following questions in complete sentences.

1.   In the first stanza what is the male elephant required to do? Answer in your own words.

2.   In the first stanza what is the female elephant made to do? Answer in your own words.

3.   What do the words (a) pallid (line 2), (b) hoary (lines 2 and 14) and (c) agog (line 5) mean?

4.   Comment on the expression 'pig-tailed monster'. Is there anything odd or unusual about it?

5.   How do the watching children react?

✎ Improve your writing

EXERCISE 3.5

Look at this verse from a nonsense poem by Lewis Carroll, 19th century author of *Alice's Adventures in Wonderland* and *Through the Looking-Glass:*

> He thought he saw an elephant,
> That practised on a fife:
> He looked again, and found it was
> A letter from his wife
> 'At length I realise' he said,
> 'The bitterness of life.'

Write your own six-line elephant nonsense poem based on this pattern.

Remember it doesn't have to make sense – the sillier the better – as long as it follows Lewis Carroll's rhyme scheme and pattern.

For example you could start:

> She thought she smelt an elephant
> Eating hot cross buns …

or

> They heard a large blue elephant
> Singing a cheerful song …

… but the best opening will be one which you make up.

 Discuss

---

EXERCISE 3.6

1. The poem 'Two Performing Elephants' is in **blank verse**. This means that it does not rhyme – or at least not regularly and formally as, for example, Tennyson's 'The Mermaid' does. It does, however, have a number of echoes at the ends of lines. These are known as **half rhymes** (sometimes called **imperfect** or **near rhymes**). Find the number of lines which end in a word ending with '-m'. What effect do you think these half rhymes have on the poem as a whole?

2. Notice how many other words in the poem end in '-m' – or have an 'm' sound. It is as if DH Lawrence wants to build a humming sound into the poem. Why do think he has done this?

3. In the poem, the poet has also used a number of 's' sounds – known as **sibilance**. Identify and talk about the sibilant words in the poem.

4. Pick three words from the poem which interest you, apart from the 'humming and hissing' ones we have already looked at. Explain to a partner why you chose them.

5. Two things particularly strike the poet about watching the elephants:
   - their ancient appearance
   - the reaction of the watching children.

   What else is he saying?

 Explore poetry further

Write a poem of your own in blank verse about animals you have observed – tame or wild – in some sort of action. Have you ever watched, for example, a cat stalking birds, a dog being trained or a wild bird on a bird feeder?

Read some other poetry by DH Lawrence such as 'Snake' or 'Mountain Lion'.

Grammar and punctuation

Commas for lists

Commas are used to separate items in a list within a sentence. You do not need a comma between the last two items when you use 'and' or 'or'.

For example:

- ... everything he saw, heard, felt, smelt or touched ...
- ... he looked about him, he munched melons, he ate bananas and he crunched sugar-cane ...
- ... melon rinds, banana skins and sugar-cane leaves ...
- ... great, grey-green, greasy Limpopo River ...

Look too at the lists in Exercise 3.3 numbers 1 and 5.

Commas acting as brackets

Commas are also put either side of words or phrases which are not essential to the main meaning of the sentence.

For example:

- He threw down the rind and leaves because, remember, he had no trunk with which to pick up his litter. ('remember' is not essential)
- There, several members of his family spoke to him. ('there' is not essential)

The commas act as brackets. (The word or words between the commas are a **parenthesis**.)

EXERCISE 3.7

Put the commas into the lists in these sentences:

1. Elephants like to eat melons bananas leaves grasses and other plants.
2. The elephant's nose was tugged yanked dragged heaved and stretched by the crocodile.
3. Near the river bank lay a clever talkative helpful and knowledgeable python.
4. Should elephants lions tigers gorillas and bears be kept in zoos?
5. You could ask your mother father sister brother aunt or uncle what they think.

EXERCISE 3.8

Read these sentences. Add words in the spaces that have commas either side of them. You can use your own words or choose from the list below:

remember   of course   however   nearby   there   you see   my child

1.   The elephant's child, _____, was insatiably curious.

2.   His relations, _____, refused to answer questions patiently.

3.   On the banks of the Limpopo, _____, a frantic struggle took place.

4.   Listen, _____, and I'll tell you a story.

5.   If you want advice, _____, ask a rock snake.

If you get that finished quickly, write six sentences of your own which need commas, either for separating items in the list or for indicating words that are not essential to the main meaning of the sentence.

Adjectives

Adjectives tell us more about nouns. We say that they **qualify** (or **modify**) nouns.

great	grey-green	greasy	tall
useful	slushy-squashy	rough	scientific

So, for example, Rudyard Kipling qualifies Limpopo (a proper noun) by telling us that it's great, grey-green and greasy; Mr Atkinson (on page 37) writes not just about research (an abstract noun) but about scientific research.

EXERCISE 3.9

Adjective activities:

1.   Play the 'Gladys's Cat' game in groups of four. The first player says, for example, 'Gladys's cat is an adventurous cat'. The second says something like 'Gladys's cat is an admirable cat,' and you take turns until everyone has said the sentence with an original adjective starting with 'a'. Then you move onto 'b': 'Gladys's cat is a bouncy cat' and so on. No repeats are allowed and you must use the whole sentence every time. The big challenge comes when you're the fourth person to get 'x'!

2. Write a poem about an animal, using strings of adjectives starting with the same letter, as Kipling uses 'great, grey-green, greasy'. You could also try to make some of them rhyme, for example 'musky tusky'.

3. Adjectives are often formed from nouns or nouns from adjectives. Fill in the adjectives on this list. The first two have been done for you:

Noun	Adjective
elephant	elephantine
bulge	bulgy
obedience	_____
thickness	_____
success	_____
curiosity	_____
naughtiness	_____
circle	_____
picture	_____

Vocabulary and spelling

1. **Elephantine** is, of course, an adjective meaning elephant-like. Find out the meanings of these adjectives: feline, aquiline, porcine, vulpine.

2. A **pachyderm** is a large animal with a thick skin such as a rhinoceros, hippopotamus or elephant. *Pakhus* is the Ancient Greek word for 'thick' and *derma* means 'skin'.

    So whenever you see 'derm' or 'derma' in a word it has probably got something to do with skin:

    ● **Dermatitis** is a skin disease.

    ● A **dermatologist** is a doctor specialising in skin problems.

    ● If you describe something as **dermatoid** you mean it looks like skin.

3. A **native** is a person or an animal who was born in a certain place, so an elephant's native land is Africa or India. If you are a native of Surrey it means that you were born there. To the Romans, who spoke and wrote Latin, the word *natus* meant 'born' and that is where this word comes from. Look out for connections in other words:

- A **nativity** play is about Jesus's birth.
- If something is **natural** to you it means you were born with the ability to do it.
- Your **nature** is the character you were born with.

Use these words in some sentences of your own.

4. Look at the spelling of **stretch**. It is quite an unusual word because it has seven letters but only one vowel. It includes 'str' and ' tch'. Can you spell these words?

strength	batch	string	fetch	strong	scratch
strung	hutch	stroll	pitch	struck	notch

Take care, by the way, with 'yacht', which looks as if it is in the same spelling family but is not.

Learn the spellings of all these words with a friend and then test each other.

Speaking and listening

1. Work in pairs. Practise reading 'The Elephant's Child' aloud together. Discuss how you are going to split it up. Then perform your reading to the rest of the class.

2. Find an animal poem. Learn it by heart. Organise a class 'poetry festival' at which you take turns to recite your poems.

3. Work with a partner. Invent a two-person play in which one of you believes that animals should be kept in zoos and the other thinks that all zoos should be closed. Work out roughly what you will say to each other. Then perform what you have practised to another pair in the class. The proper name for this work is **role play**.

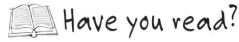 # Have you read?

The following books are all about animals:

- *Just So Stories* by Rudyard Kipling (1902)
- *The Jungle Book* by Rudyard Kipling (1894)
- *The Sheep-pig* by Dick King Smith (1983)
- *Charlotte's Web* by EB White (1952)
- *How the Whale Became* by Ted Hughes (1963)
- *The Road to Somewhere* by Helen Armstrong (2000)
- *The Road to the River* by Helen Armstrong (2001)
- *Born to Run* by Michael Morpurgo (2007)
- *Watership Down* by Richard Adams (1972)
- *Tarka the Otter* by Henry Williamson (1927)
- *Black Beauty* by Anna Sewell (1877)

✔ And if you've done all that ...

- Look up the RSPCA and World Wildlife Fund in an encyclopaedia or on the internet (www.rspca.org.uk; www.wwf.org.uk). Prepare a short talk about their work for the rest of the class.

- Read one of the last three recommended books on the reading list (they are longer than the others on the list). Tell the rest of the class about the book and what you liked or disliked about it.

- How many different ways can you think of in which human beings make use of animals? Write a list. Work out which of these you think is fair and right and which you think is not, and why. For example, you might approve of a guide dog working for a blind person but be unhappy about bull fighting. Write your views down or make them into a talk for part or all of your class.

Chapter 4 The Second World War

A discovery

Chas McGill collects war souvenirs. It is the winter of 1940/1. Tyneside, where Chas lives, is being relentlessly bombed by the Germans.

1   The wood was bleak and ugly too. Grown-ups dumped rubbish round the outside, and kids climbed and broke the trees. But nobody went into the middle. Some said it was haunted but Chas had never found anything there but a feeling of cold misery, which wasn't exciting like a headless horseman.

5   Still, it was an oddly discouraging sort of place.

Every year the briars grew thicker. Even Chas knew only one way through them. He took it now, wriggling under the arches of briar as thick as your finger, interlaced like barbed wire. He picked himself up quickly because the grass was soaking. The sky seemed greyer through the bare branches and he

10   felt fed up. Still, since he was here he might as well search for souvenirs.

He sniffed. There was a funny, foreign smell in the wood … like petrol and fireworks. Funny – it wasn't Guy Fawkes yet. Some kids must have been messing about. As he pressed on, the smell grew stronger. There must be an awful lot of petrol.

15   Something was blocking out the light through the branches. A new building; a secret army base; a new anti-aircraft gun? He couldn't quite see except that it was black.

And then he saw, quite clearly at the top, a swastika[1], black – outlined in white. He didn't know whether to run towards it or away. So he stayed

20   stock-still, listening. Not a sound. He moved forward again.

He burst into the clearing. It was the tail of the German aircraft which had crashed on the laundry. At least, most of it had crashed on the laundry. The tail, breaking off in the air, had spun to earth like a sycamore seed. He'd read of that happening in books. He could also tell from books that this had been

25   a *Heinkel He 111*[2].

Chas sighed. If he reported it, they'd just come and take it away for scrap. Like when he'd taken that shiny new incendiary-bomb rack to the Warden's post … they'd not even said thank you.

Chas gulped. The machine gun was still there, hanging from the turret, shiny

30   and black.

He reached up and
tugged at the round
gun barrel. Then he
grabbed it, put his
35 plimsolls against the
curving side of the
plane and went up
like a monkey. He
peered over the
40 edge of the cockpit.

The gunner was
sitting there
watching him. One
hand, in a soft fur
45 mitt, was stretched
up as if to retrieve
the gun. The other
lay in his overalled
lap. He wore the
50 black leather flying
helmet of the
Luftwaffe[3] and
goggles. His right
eye, pale grey,
55 watched through
the goggle glass

tolerantly and a little sadly. He looked a nice man, young.

The glass of the other goggle was gone. Its rim was thick with sticky red.
Inside was a seething mass of black flies, which rose and buzzed angrily at
60 Chas's arrival, then sank back into the goggle again.

For a terrible moment, Chas thought the Nazi was alive, that the mitted
hand would reach out and grab him. Then, even worse, he knew he was
dead.

Slightly adapted from *The Machine Gunners* by Robert Westall (1975)

Notes:
[1] A squared-off cross used by Nazi Germany as a logo or symbol
[2] A German bomber
[3] The German air force

EXERCISE 4.1

Read the extract from *The Machine Gunners* and answer the following questions in full sentences.

1. How does Robert Westall make the wood seem sinister even before Chas finds the aircraft tail?

2. What is the first sign that there is something unusual to be found in the wood?

3. What does Chas mainly want from the aircraft?

4. Why does Westall tell us that the German gunner was watching Chas when later he tells us that the man was dead?

5. Why does the author use the word 'tolerantly' when describing how the pilot's eye looked through the glass?

6. Give another word for (a) interlaced (line 8), (b) peered (line 39) and (c) retrieve (line 46).

Utility clothing

A group of people in the Milton Keynes area of Buckinghamshire have investigated life in the Second World War (1939–45) and talked to those who remember it about their experience and memories. The results of their project are on www.livingarchive.org.uk This is what they have uncovered about clothes of the 1940s.

1   The clothing industry was a lot smaller during the war and clothes became more expensive. To make sure everyone could afford them, the government introduced 'Utility Clothing'. This was made from a particular cloth and cut in a special way so only the smallest amount was used.

5   Clothing rationing was introduced in June 1941 and operated on a 'points' basis. Each person was allowed 66 clothing coupons a year. For example:

    Man's suit – 26 coupons

    Woollen dress – 11 coupons

    Child's shoes – 3 coupons

10 People were encouraged to 'make do and mend' by the government who

suggested ways to revamp old clothes. Patching and darning meant clothes could be worn for longer.

Boys aged 4–14 in the 1930s and '40s would normally have worn:

    Short trousers

15   Shirt and tie (usually a knitted school tie)

    V-necked jumper

    Jacket or school blazer

    Long socks

20   Sandals or boots

Girls aged 4–14 in the 1930s and '40s would normally have worn:

    Cotton frock (dress) in summer

    Gym-slip and blouse in winter

    Cardigan or jumper

25   School beret or hat

    Long socks or lisle[1] stockings

    Sandals or shoes

Monica Austin remembers: 'We used to have Thermojene inside our clothes. It was a kind of orange cotton wool, stronger than cotton wool but

30   it kept the warmth on your chest. We used to put it down as we got dressed to keep us warm.'

From www.livingarchive.org.uk

Note:
[1] A type of thread

EXERCISE 4.2

Read the information on 'utility clothing' and answer the following questions in full sentences.

1. What was 'utility clothing' (line 3)?

2. What did people do to make their clothes last longer?

3. Explain in your own words what Thermojene was (line 28).

4. Why do you think the government introduced a 'points' system?

5. What would Chas McGill probably have been wearing (see page 47)?

✎ Your turn to write

EXERCISE 4.3

1. Chas McGill collected war souvenirs. Write in any way you wish about something that you collect.

2. Write about an occasion when you saw or found something which surprised, frightened or puzzled you.

3. Describe in detail, and in your own words, the appearance of a ten-year-old school girl or boy in the 1940s. Introduce extra details to make your writing as lively as possible.

4. Imagine you are a journalist on Chas McGill's local paper. You have interviewed him about his find in the wood. Write your report for the paper.

5. Write in any way you wish about war.

✎ Improve your writing

EXERCISE 4.4

You are going to write a short letter (or email) to a newspaper expressing your view about how the Second World War is taught in schools, other ways in which young people learn about it and why it matters.

1. Jot down in note form the points you want to make, including names of novels such as *The Machine Gunners* from which children learn about the Second World War.

2. Think of a strong opening sentence which summarises what you want to say.

3. Think of a punchy concluding sentence. A question often works well at the end of a letter to a newspaper.

4. Write your letter in rough.

5. Edit it very strictly. Cut out any word or phrase which does not add to your argument or which is repetitive.

6. Check spelling, grammar and punctuation carefully.

7. Produce your final draft.

8. You've worked hard on your letter or email, and made some interesting points. If you have the permission of your teacher or parents, you could send it to a newspaper. An editor just might think it worthy of publication.

'Earlswood'

Fleur Adcock was born in New Zealand but spent much of her childhood, including the years of the Second World War, in England.

1
Air-raid shelters at school were damp tunnels
where you sang 'Ten Green Bottles' yet again
and might as well have been doing decimals.

At home, though, it was cosier and more fun:
5
cocoa and toast inside the Table Shelter,
our iron panelled bunker, our new den.

By day we ate off it; at night you'd find us
under it, the floor plump with mattresses
and the wire grilles neatly latched around us.

10   You had to be careful not to bump your head;
        we padded the hard metal bits with pillows,
        then giggled in our glorious social bed.

        What could be safer? What could be more romantic
        than playing cards by torchlight in a raid?
15   Odd that it made our mother so neurotic

        to hear the sirens; we were quite content
        but slightly cramped once there were four of us,
        after we'd taken in old Mrs Brent

        from down by the Nag's Head, who'd been bombed out.
20   She had her arm in plaster but she managed
        to dress herself, and smiled, and seemed all right.

        Perhaps I just imagined hearing her
        moaning a little in the night, and shaking
        splinters of glass out of her long grey hair.

25   The next week we were sent to Leicestershire.

        Fleur Adcock (1986)

EXERCISE 4.5

1. We learn that Mrs Brent:
    - lived near the Nag's Head
    - has lost her home because of bombing
    - has a broken arm but can dress herself
    - smiles
    - moans in the night and is clearly distressed by her experiences
    - has long grey hair
    - thinks there are fragments of broken glass in her hair
    - is not understood by the child at the centre of the poem.

    Put these facts in order of importance.

2. From whose point of view is this poem written?

    (a)   a child   (b)   an adult looking back on childhood

    (c)   a neurotic mother   (d)   an old lady who has been 'bombed out'

3. What do you learn from the poem about the child's mother?

4. Who are the four people mentioned in the sixth verse?

5. What is the connection between Mrs Brent's arrival and the evacuation to Leicestershire?

 Discuss

EXERCISE 4.6

1. Look carefully at how the poem is arranged. It consists of eight 3-line verses and then an abrupt single line – like an unexpected chord at the end of a piece of music. Now look at the rhyme scheme. How has the poet used rhyme?

2. As in DH Lawrence's 'Two Elephants Performing' most of the rhymes at the ends of lines are half rhymes. What, if anything, does the rhyme add to the poem?

3. The rhyme is not very obvious. How aware of it are you when you read or hear the poem?

4. Is there any sort of regular beat or rhythm in this poem? In pairs or small groups, try:
    ● counting the number of syllables in each line
    ● writing out a verse or two as if it were prose (without line breaks) to see what difference it makes to the effect the poem has on you.

5. The fifth verse does not end in a full stop because its meaning is carried into the sixth verse. Similarly the sixth verse ends part-way through a sentence which is completed in the seventh verse. This is called **enjambement**.

    What effect does the enjambement have in the poem? Does it:
    ● Make it flow more freely and naturally like someone remembering?
    ● Make the poem move faster towards the end? If so, why?
    ● Have some other effect?

⊕ Explore poetry further

Find and read some other poetry by Fleur Adcock (born 1934).

Prepare a performance of 'Earlswood' for the rest of the class – perhaps learning the poem by heart. Think very carefully about how you will speak each line.

Grammar and punctuation

Exclamation marks

An exclamation mark (!) draws attention to a sentence which is more dramatic than a plain sentence which ends in a full stop. It is often used to show that the sentence is (or is supposed to be) funny. It should not be used too often. Do not use more than one at a time, and remember, an exclamation mark stands on its own. You don't need any other mark of punctuation with it.

For example:

- My teacher came to school wearing a green wig!
- There are seven girls named Charlotte in my class!
- I have read *The Machine Gunners* eleven times!
- What a lovely book!

You also need an exclamation mark after a single word or short exclamation such as:

Cool!   Great!   Oh dear!   Good heavens!

EXERCISE 4.7

Exclamation mark activities:

1.   Punctuate the following exclamations:

   (a) stop thief
   (b) what a terrible story
   (c) how hot the weather is
   (d) you poor child
   (e) what a shame
   (f) how lovely

2. Write out the following, correctly punctuated. Some are exclamations. Some are ordinary sentences.

   (a) he wanted to find the source of the smell

   (b) how few clothes those children had in the 1940s

   (c) no don't do that

   (d) most girls wore berets

   (e) mending clothes made them last

   (f) what a smell

   (g) ouch

Adverbs

An adverb is a word which tells you more about another word, usually a verb or an adjective. It **qualifies** or **modifies** it. Adverbs often tell you **how** or **when** something happened. Many adverbs, but not all, end in '-ly'. For example:

- He picked himself up **quickly**.
- His right eye, pale grey, watched through the goggle glass, **tolerantly** and a little **sadly**.
- Monica Austin remembers Thermojene **well**.
- I shall do my prep **soon**.

EXERCISE 4.8

Adverb activities:

1. Put adverbs into these sentences:

   (a) Chas McGill entered the wood _____ and searched _____ for souvenirs.

   (b) During the war everyone had to dress _____.

   (c) Many people are now _____ interested in the Second World War.

   (d) Children in the war were _____ advised to keep away from aircraft and weapons.

   (e) Some older people _____ remember Second World War bombing raids _____.

   (f) Rationing was a way of sharing things out _____.

2. Most adjectives (see Chapter 3) which qualify or modify nouns can be converted into adverbs which qualify or modify verbs. Make these adjectives into adverbs and use each adverb in a sentence of your own.

Adjective	Adverb
normal	_____
good	well
funny	funnily
bad	_____
expensive	_____
frightening	_____
public	publicly
clear	_____
warm	_____
easy	_____

Vocabulary and spelling

1. **Utility** means usefulness. During the Second World War people were encouraged to buy specially made cheap and simple utility furniture and other items, as well as clothing.

   A **utility room** in a house is one where useful jobs such as washing clothes are done. In sport a **utility player** is one who can usefully play well in any one of several positions.

   Futility means uselessness or without usefulness.

2. **Thermojene** was the name give to a substance which helped to keep people warm in the 1940s. Any word containing 'therm' has something to do with heat. It comes from *thermos*, the Ancient Greek word for 'heat'.

   A **thermometer** measures heat.

   Thermal clothing keeps you especially warm.

   A **thermos** flask is a special container which keeps liquids hot, perhaps for picnics.

   Look in a good dictionary for many other – mainly scientific – words containing 'therm'.

3. Look at the spelling of **retrieve**. The 'i' comes before the 'e' because the sound that it is making is 'eee' as in 'feel', not 'aii' as in 'file'. Learn these:

achieve	believe	relief	niece	piece
field	siege	pier	thief	grief

But beware! When a 'c' comes first, the 'e' and 'i' change places. So:

conceit   deceive   receive   ceiling

But note that this rule only applies when the sound is 'eee', as in the words above.

4. When you form an adverb from an adjective ending with a '-y' the rule is that the 'y' changes to an 'i' before 'ly' is added.

So:

funny	funnily
merry	merrily
happy	happily
silky	silkily
hungry	hungrily

Remember: Change 'y' to 'i' and add 'ly'.

Collect and list as many examples of this rule as you can.

Speaking and listening

1. Read one or more of the books listed opposite. Read a short extract from it aloud to your class and tell the class what you liked or disliked about the book.

2. Working with a partner, make up a conversation between a child of your age from the 1940s and one from the 21st century. Talk about what you each do in your spare time, what you wear and anything else that interests you. Then perform your conversation to the rest of the class.

3. Discuss war in groups. When, if ever, is it right? When, if ever, is it wrong? Why do people go to war? What effect does it have on

ordinary people across the world? A spokesperson for your group could then explain your group's views to the rest of the class.

 # Have you read?

All these are about children and how they were affected by the Second World War in Britain and elsewhere:

- *The Machine Gunners* by Robert Westall (1975)
- *Back Home* by Michelle Magorian (1984)
- *The Diary of a Young Girl* by Anne Frank (1947)
- *Carrie's War* by Nina Bawden (1973)
- *Fireweed* by Jill Paton Walsh (1969)
- *The Silver Sword* by Ian Seraillier (1956)
- *August '44* by Carlo Gebler (2003)
- *Mischling, Second Degree* by Ilse Koehn (1977)
- *The Endless Steppe* by Esther Hautzig (1968)
- *The Exeter Blitz* by David Rees (1978)
- *Ronnie's War* by Bernard Ashley (2010)

✔ And if you've done all that ...

- Sir Winston Churchill was Britain's Prime Minister during the Second World War. He made some very famous speeches to encourage people to be strong. They were broadcast on radio. Download or request a CD of these speeches (from your local library or www.churchill-society-london.org.uk). What do you learn from them about (a) how British people must then have been feeling; and (b) Churchill's personality?

- Find out what you can about Robert Westall who wrote *The Machine Gunners*. Write a short account of his life and work for display in your classroom.

- Look through some anthologies of 20th century poetry to find poems about the Second World War. Write some of them out to form your own anthology.

Chapter 5 Shakespeare

Back in time

Nat Field is an American boy who has come to London in 1999 to take part in a children's production of Shakespeare's *A Midsummer Night's Dream* at the new Globe Theatre. Taken seriously ill, he finds himself transported back to the old Globe Theatre four hundred years earlier.

1   'There it is – our new theatre!' said Harry proudly. 'Hast seen it before?'

'No,' I said truthfully, staring. A white flag was flying from the flagpole on top of the Globe, the signal to audiences that a play would be done there that day. For the moment, it was the only thing I recognised. It wasn't the theatre

5   itself that was so startlingly different from the copy that would be built in my time; it was the surroundings. This Globe wasn't crowded and dwarfed by towering office buildings; it stood up proud and high, and

10   to the south it looked out over green fields and billowing trees. In fact there were

15   trees nearly all round it; once we had left the main street that went over London Bridge,

20   I'd felt, with astonishment, that we were walking into the countryside. The streets were

25   still busy and noisy, though, with carts and coaches and horsemen, and others like us

30   bustling on foot.

Like the Globe of my own time, the theatre looked new; its plaster gleamed white, the reeds of its thatch lay tight and straight-edged. As Harry chattered proudly on, the apprentice of the Lord Chamberlain's Men explaining his company to the borrowed boy from St Paul's School, I

35 realised that it really was new, finished only a few months earlier. Before that, the company had been playing for years in a theatre – called, believe it or not, just The Theatre – across the river, in Shoreditch, until their lease on the land ran out and the landlord refused to renew it. Master Burbage and his brother Cuthbert had just inherited The Theatre from their father

40 James, who built it. There it stood, useless, on ground they weren't allowed to set foot on. Where were they to act?

It was the actors who solved the problem, Harry said, grinning. Five of them got together with the Burbages, raised enough money to lease a piece of land here in Southwark, and hired a master carpenter. ('My uncle,' said

45 Harry possessively. 'His name is Peter Streete.') Then, one dark winter's night just after Christmas, taking a dozen strong workmen with them, they went quietly to Shoreditch and with axes and sledgehammers and crowbars they took The Theatre apart. They did it very carefully, numbering each piece, and it took them three days. The demolition must have been a very

50 noisy process, but Harry said not many people lived in the area close by.

After that they carted all the Theatre's major beams and timbers to the river Thames – huge oak beams, Harry said, some of them thirty feet long – and shipped them over to the other side. And there, using them for a framework, Peter Streete and his workmen gradually built the theatre that

55 they christened the Globe.

Birds were singing in the trees outside the theatre as we went in. The doors seemed smaller than in my day, and in different places, so that I couldn't tell whether we were headed backstage or for the groundlings' pit. I followed Harry and Burbage blindly, through narrow passages, past busy pre-occupied

60 men and boys; the whole theatre had an odd musty, grassy smell that I couldn't place, and everywhere of course there were the unfamiliar accents and clothes. To keep from thinking I was crazy, I'd begun to pretend that I was in the middle of a movie set in Elizabethan times, among actors dressed in costume. It was comforting until something screamingly real hit me, like

65 those heads over London Bridge.

Two boys hurried past us, paused, and looked back, calling to Harry, and I went quickly on after Master Burbage, who was climbing a narrow staircase.

From somewhere beyond it came the sound of voices, indistinct but loud, one of them very loud, as if angry.

70 There was bright light ahead of us all at once. Master Burbage paused, and I found we had come out on to the central little balcony at the back of the stage. I had to step over a coil of thick rope lying on the balcony floor, and saw one end of it tied firmly to the balcony rail; it was a knotted climbing-rope for a quick descent to the stage, something Arby had planned to use
75 in my own time. I might have thought myself still in my own time if it hadn't been for Master Burbage at my side. Ahead and around us were the empty galleries of the theatre; above us the painted sky of the 'heavens' that gave the stage its roof and below, on the broad thrusting stage, two figures, arguing.

From *King of Shadows* by Susan Cooper (1999)

EXERCISE 5.1

Read the extract from *King of Shadows* and answer the following questions in full sentences.

1. List three differences Nat notices between the 20th century Globe Theatre he knows and the old one he has been transported back to.

2. Who built The Theatre in Shoreditch?

3. Why could The Theatre no longer be used?

4. Give another word for (a) demolition (line 49) and (b) musty (line 60).

5. In order to travel from Shoreditch to Southwark what must you cross?

6. Why do the people in the theatre look and sound odd to Nat?

Rebuilding Shakespeare's Globe

1   The project to rebuild Shakespeare's Globe was initiated by the American actor, director and producer Sam Wanamaker after his first visit to London in 1949. Twenty-one years later he founded what was to become the Shakespeare Globe Trust, dedicated to the reconstruction of the theatre

5   and the creation of an education centre and permanent exhibition.

After 23 years spent tirelessly fundraising, advancing research into the appearance of the original Globe and planning the reconstruction with the Trust's architect Theo Crosby, Sam Wanamaker died. The site had been secured. The exhibition

10   undercroft was structurally complete and a few timber bays of the theatre were in place. Three and a half years later the theatre was completed.

15   What did the first Globe look like? Nobody knows for sure. Printed panoramas, such as those by John Norden and Wenceslaus Hollar, give some idea of the theatre's exterior. Written accounts, usually by

20   visitors from overseas, building contracts and one sketch (of the Swan theatre) tell us something about the interior.

Techniques used in the reconstruction of the theatre were painstakingly accurate. 'Green' oak was cut and fashioned according to 16th century practice and assembled in two-dimensional bays on the Bankside site. Oak

25   laths and staves support lime plaster mixed according to a contemporary recipe and the walls are covered in a white lime wash. The roof is made of water reed thatch.

The new Globe is also designed with the 21st century in mind. An additional exit, illuminated signage, fire retardant materials and some

30   modern backstage machinery are all concessions to our times.

The reconstruction is as faithful to the original as modern scholarship and traditional craftsmanship can make it, but for the time being this Globe is – and is likely to remain – neither more nor less than the 'best guess' at Shakespeare's theatre.

Slightly adapted from www.shakespearesglobe.com

EXERCISE 5.2

Read the extract 'Rebuilding Shakespeare's Globe' and answer the following questions in full sentences.

1. Whose idea was it to rebuild Shakespeare's Globe in late 20th century London?

2. For how long did he work on plans for Shakespeare's Globe?

3. Whose drawings of the original Globe helped to show what it looked like?

4. In what ways did the building of the replica Globe copy old building methods?

5. What features are included to make sure the building meets modern health and safety standards?

Your turn to write

EXERCISE 5.3

1. Write a story about someone who moves to a time other than his or her own.

2. Imagine you are a journalist interviewing Nat Field when he returns to the present day. Write your article for a newspaper or magazine.

3. Write on the subject of theatre in any way you wish.

4. Write a review for a newspaper or magazine of any play, musical, pantomime or film you have seen recently. Include how it was done, which actors did well and which less well. Say what you liked and disliked about the production.

5. Write an account of any school (or other) play you have taken part in. Include as much detail as you can. For example: How did you rehearse? How did you feel when you got your part? What were the costumes like? How did it go when you performed it for an audience?

✎ Improve your writing

EXERCISE 5.4

Write a dramatic paragraph describing something which happened in a play (or film or TV drama) which you have seen. Use some of the following words:

sinister	eerie	disturbing	evocative	melodramatic
powerful	unconvincing	hilarious	comic	dramatic

You might also need specialist theatre vocabulary such as:

upstage	rostrum	wings	backstage	trap
footlights	set	proscenium	orchestra pit	fly tower

'Sonnet 91'

This 14-line poem is a sonnet. Shakespeare wrote 154 of them and they were published during his lifetime. All Shakespeare's sonnets are love poems of some sort. No one knows who they were written for, but we can tell they were not all addressed to the same person.

1   Some glory in their birth, some their skill,
     Some in their wealth, some their body's force,
     Some in their garments, through new-fangled ill,
     Some in their hawks and hounds, some in their horse;
5   And every humour has his adjunct pleasure,
     Wherein it finds a joy above the rest;
     But these particulars are not my measure:
     All these I better in one general best.
     Thy love is better than high birth to me,
10   Richer than wealth, prouder than garments' cost,
     Of more delight than hawks or horses be;
     And having thee, of all men's pride I boast:
        Wretched in this alone, that thou mayst take
        All this away and me most wretched make.

William Shakespeare (1609)

This painting by Robert Dudley depicts a scene from Shakespeare's *Romeo and Juliet*; a tragic love story

EXERCISE 5.5

Read 'Sonnet 91' and answer the following questions in full sentences.

1.   List three things which the poet notices that people take pride in.

2.   What does the word 'humour' mean in this context? (It is different from its modern meaning.) Use a dictionary to help you.

3.   Give another word for (a) new-fangled (line 3), (b) adjunct (line 5) and (c) wretched (line 13).

 Discuss

EXERCISE 5.6

1.   What is this sonnet really about? (The clue is in the ninth line.)

2.   In a pair, or a small group, work out the rhyme scheme of this sonnet. Call the first line A, the second B – and so on.

3.   What are the things, according to the poet, which are *not* important in life compared with love for a friend.

4.   Look at the last two lines. What is the speaker's greatest worry?

5.   There is a lot of repetition in this sonnet. Look at the poem carefully to work out where the repetition comes. Do you think it:

   ● Emphasises the poet's strong feelings?
   ● Makes the poem dull?
   ● Adds to the effect of the poem?

6.   Write a version of the sonnet using your own words to express the same ideas and feelings. Which version do you prefer and why?

Explore poetry further

Find and read some more of Shakespeare's sonnets. Numbers 18, 116 and 130 are particularly appealing.

You could try writing a sonnet of your own using Shakespeare's rhyme scheme.

Grammar and punctuation

Adjectives from nouns

Nouns and adjectives are often versions of the same word:

Noun	Adjective
theatre	theatrical
Britain	British
bird	birdlike
grass	grassy
history	historical
education	educational

There are patterns that you can see, but great care needs to be taken with the spelling. For example, in many cases we add 'ful' (note *one* 'l', not two):

truth	truthful
wonder	wonderful
cheer	cheerful

Or we can add 'y' (or 'ly'):

craft	crafty
love	lovely
noise	noisy

These patterns are easy enough for people who have been speaking English all their lives, but pity those who have to learn English as a foreign language. Truthful? Truthy? Truthlike? Truthly? Not easy!

EXERCISE 5.7

Noun/adjective activities:

1. Write a list of as many nouns ending in -iness as you can. Then list corresponding adjectives based on them. For example, 'happiness' and 'happy'.

2. Write a list of as many adjectives ending in '-y' as you can. Then list corresponding nouns next to them. For example, 'angry' and 'anger'.

3. Put the right noun or adjective in the following sentences:

   (a) The Globe is a (carefulness/careful) replica of an (Elizabethan/Elizabeth) building.

   (b) We can understand the (popular/popularity) of (Shakespeare/Shakespearian) drama.

   (c) Nat Field was surprised by the (atmosphere/atmospheric) of Tudor London.

   (d) Shakespeare was (English/England).

   (e) Oak is a very (hardness/hard) and (reliable/reliability) wood.

Hyphens

A hyphen is a small horizontal line which separates two or more linked words, or parts of a word. When we use more than one word to form a single idea we need a hyphen:

- pre-war theatre
- under-11 netball team
- end-of-term report

Hyphens change the way we say things. Practise saying aloud: 'Let's take away that rubbish!' and 'Let's get a take-away supper!' Can you hear the difference?
Hyphens also make meaning clearer. For example:

- King Henry VIII married his sister-in-law.
- Nat Field was a 12-year-old boy when he came to London.
- Prince Charles is an ex-naval officer.

EXERCISE 5.8

Put hyphens into these sentences:

1. We put on a play with a five person cast.
2. King James I of England was a non smoker.
3. In Shakespeare's play *Hamlet*, Claudius is Gertrude's brother in law as well as her new husband and Hamlet's stepfather.
4. *Henry V* by Shakespeare, written in 1599, was a turn of the century play.
5. Queen Victoria's end of reign celebration was her Diamond Jubilee in 1897 when she had been monarch for 60 years.
6. Shakespeare lived in Stratford upon Avon.

Dashes

All sentences must have a capital letter at the beginning and a full stop, question or exclamation mark at the end, but you can sometimes use a dash within the sentence to break up the meaning. A dash looks like a long hyphen but is not attached to a particular word.

For example:

- There it is – our new theatre.
- Queen Victoria had nine children – then her husband died.
- Charles I upset his subjects – so they beheaded him.

EXERCISE 5.9

Put dashes into these sentences:

1. The Globe Theatre was magnificent but it burned down.
2. Shakespeare's Macbeth was very ambitious although audiences usually think he was led on by his wife.
3. Sam Wanamaker worked for years on the Globe Theatre project but died before it was finished.
4. Queen Elizabeth I encouraged playwrights but she never went to the theatre.

Dashes (continued)

You can use dashes in pairs, like brackets:

- William Shakespeare – a remarkable playwright – wrote both tragedies and comedies.

- A magnificent palace on the Thames – Hampton Court – was given to Henry VIII by Thomas Wolsey.

Vocabulary and spelling

1. When the theatre was dismantled, craftsmen had to number the pieces carefully. The following adverbs are similar in meaning to carefully:

    scrupulously   delicately   meticulously

    attentively   painstakingly

    Look up their precise meaning and use them in sentences of your own.

2. If you **initiate** something, as Sam Wanamaker did for the project to build the new Globe Theatre, you **start** it.

    Look up and list short (one sound or one syllable) words for the following longer ones:

    veracity   peregrination   endeavour   obtain   purchase   ingest

    A famous newspaper editor, Harold Evans, advised his writers never to use a long word where a short one would do. It is good advice. Although you need to know the meaning of as many longer words as possible, it is often more effective to use the shortest possible one in your writing.

3. Many abstract nouns end in -ness but take care with the spelling of two groups.

    (a) If the adjective from which the noun is formed ends in '-n' then adding 'ness' means that the word is spelt with a double 'n'.

         For example: 'open' becomes 'openness' and 'clean' becomes 'cleanness'.

         Learn these:

sternness	suddenness
drunkenness	keenness
sullenness	meanness
leanness	greenness
thinness	woodenness

(b)   If the adjective from which the noun is formed ends in '-y' then the 'y' changes to an 'i' before 'ness' is added.

For example: 'tiny' becomes 'tininess' and 'fussy' becomes 'fussiness'.

Learn these:

tidiness	silliness
happiness	noisiness
crankiness	worthiness
dizziness	weariness
readiness	sulkiness

Speaking and listening

1. Work in a group. Make up a short play in which a modern person meets one or more characters from the past.

2. Shakespeare wrote 154 sonnets (14-line poems). Find one which you like. Practise reading it aloud. Hold a class 'sonnet festival' in which you all perform your sonnets.

3. Work out your own short version of the story of any of Shakespeare's plays. Retell it to a small group.

4. Prepare a short talk for the rest of the class on any aspect of theatre history or theatre buildings.

Have you read?

All these are about the theatre, plays or Shakespeare:

- *King of Shadows* by Susan Cooper (1999)
- *Stratford Boys* by Jan Mark (2003)
- *The Swish of the Curtain* by Pamela Brown (1941)
- *Shakespeare Stories* by Leon Garfield (1985)
- *Shakespeare Stories II* by Leon Garfield (1994)
- *The Dark Behind the Curtain* by Gillian Cross (1982)
- *Ballet Shoes* by Noel Streatfeild (1936)
- *Theatre Shoes* by Noel Streatfeild (1945)
- *A Spoonful of Jam* by Michelle Magorian (1998)
- *Stagestruck* by Adèle Geras (1999)
- *Lights, Camera, Action!* by Adèle Geras (2000)

✔ And if you've done all that ...

- In the extract from *King of Shadows*, Nat Field remembered 'those heads on London Bridge' (line 65). Find out what this refers to. Use reference books or the internet. Share what you find out with the rest of the class.

- Find out how many plays Shakespeare wrote. Design a large poster listing them all, or most of them, with a sentence or two and an illustration for each. Work out how best to group or list them. Display it in the classroom or elsewhere in the school. (Leon Garfield's books could help with this. See 'Have you read?' on page 71.)

- Read, or try to see a production or film of, *A Midsummer Night's Dream*. Then design costumes and sets for an imaginative production of your own.

Chapter 6 Fantasy

The Minotaur

Phoenix is exploring the Greek myth 'Theseus and the Minotaur' in a very realistic and dangerous way.

1   But still the beast stood in the archway, pawing at the floor. It was bigger than a man. It stood almost three metres tall and was massively built with slabs of muscle on its chest and shoulders. Below the waist it was bull-like. It had a swinging tail and mud-splattered hooves. Or was it mud? Above the

5   waist it was a man, except, that is, for the head. And what a head! The muzzle was huge and when it opened, it revealed the sharp, curved teeth, not of a bull but of a big cat. They were the fangs of a lion or tiger made for ripping flesh. Its eyes were yellow and blazed unflinchingly through the murk. Then there were the great horns, glinting and sharp, curving from its

10 monstrous brow. Thick and muscular as the neck was, it seemed barely able to support such a fearsome head, and strained visibly under the

15 impossible weight.

'Oh my!'

The beast stepped out from the tunnel and the boy actually took a few steps back. It was as if his soul

20 had crept out of his body and was tugging at him, begging him to get away. In the sparse light shed from the gratings in the ceiling the beast looked even more hideous. There

25 was sweat for a start, standing out in gleaming beads on that enormous neck and shoulders.

But that wasn't all. The creature was smeared from head to foot with filth

30 and dried blood. It was every inch a killer. The beast began to stamp

forward, its hooves clashing on the stone floor. It raised its head, the horns scraping on the ceiling and gave a bellow that seemed to crush the air.

'I can't do this …'

35 He fell back, scrambling over the obstacles on the floor and fled. That's when he realised he'd dropped his ball of string. His lifeline had gone.

'Oh no!'

The beast was charging head down.

Got to get out of here!

40 In his mind's eye, he could see himself impaled on the points of those evil-looking horns, his legs pedalling feebly in the air, his head snapped back, his eyes growing pale and lifeless.

Suddenly he was running for his life, skidding on the slimy floor.

* * * * * *

Ripping off the mask and gloves, Phoenix bent double, gulping down air like
45 it had been rationed. The dank half-light of the tunnels was replaced by the welcome glow from an Anglepoise lamp in his father's study. He glanced at the score bracelet on his wrist. It registered total defeat: **000000**. For a few moments everything was spinning, the claws of the game digging into the flesh of the here and now. Then his surroundings became reassuringly familiar.

50 He was out. It was a game.

'Well?' his dad asked. 'What do you think?'

'Mind-blowing,' Phoenix panted. 'It was all so real. It was like another world. I mean I was Theseus. I went into the palace of the tyrant-king Minos. I could actually touch the stone columns, feel the heat of the braziers, smell
55 the incense.'

He knew he was gushing, babbling like a little kid, but he didn't care. 'The king's daughter Ariadne helped me and she wasn't just an image on a screen. She was a real girl. Then I actually came face to face with the Minotaur. It was really happening. I believed it,' he shivered. 'Still do.'

60 'Oh I could tell how convincing it was,' said Dad, enjoying the mixture of excitement and fear in his son's voice. 'You were screaming your silly head off by the end. I bet your mother thought I was killing you in here.'

From *Shadow of the Minotaur* by Alan Gibbons (2000)

EXERCISE 6.1

Read the extract from *Shadow of the Minotaur* and answer the following questions in full sentences.

1. Describe the beast as accurately as you can using your own words.

2. Who is Ariadne?

3. Give another word for (a) sparse (line 22), (b) impaled (line 40) and (c) braziers (line 54).

4. Phoenix experiences the beast's world with four of his five senses (sight, hearing, touch, smell). How do we know this?

5. How did Phoenix feel when he found himself in his father's study?

6. Why did the score bracelet show a row of zeros (or noughts) (line 47)?

Fantastic Mr Fox: a review

This is a theatre review. The author, Nuala Calvi, has seen a play and written her views in a newspaper.

1   **Fantastic Mr Fox**
    Little Angel Theatre, London, 11th September–7th November, 2010
    Author: Roald Dahl, adapted by Sarah Woods
    Director: Steve Tiplady
5   Producer: Little Angel Theatre
    Cast: Charlie Folorunsho, Rachel Leonard, Andrea Sadler,
                     Mark Whitaker
    Running time: 1hr 20mins

    After Wes Anderson's 2009 film version re-imagined the foxy first family of
10 children's fiction as a dysfunctional all-American clan, it's a relief to return
    to the unadulterated Englishness of Roald Dahl's creation.

    This *Fantastic Mr Fox*, in the capable hands of the Little Angel puppet
    theatre's associate director Steve Tiplady and adapter Sarah Woods, doesn't
    try so hard to lace the classic story with a knowing adult humour. The odd
15 quip may be there for the grown-ups, but in the main the play rolls joyfully

in the muddy world of Dahl's imagination – Farmer Bean's stinky breath, Farmer Boggis' fondness for "mashed-up duck liver smashed into doughnuts" – which tickles children's funny bones so perfectly.

20 Completed by the hapless Bunce, the trio of gun-toting landowner puppets – who lay siege to the foxes after losing one chicken too many – are delightfully disgusting, with their stringy hair, raggedy clothes and manky habits.

They rather out-perform the creatures we're rooting for beneath their feet who, with their box-like bodies and angular, card features, don't have the 25 furry appeal of either real animals or children's toys.

Otherwise, Peter O'Rourke's design is wonderfully inventive, the set a higgledy-piggledy 2D creation which nods to the show's storybook origins and gradually sheds layer upon layer as the foxes dig themselves to safety, revealing new nooks and crannies for the performance to continue.

30 An energetic cast is led by Charlie Folorunsho as the titular father figure, whose smooth renditions of composer Ben Glasstone's bluesy, witty, musical numbers are among the show's highlights. Forget George Clooney and multimillion dollar budgets – this production is easily more fantastic.

From an article by Nuala Calvi published on the website of *The Stage* and later in the paper (2010)

EXERCISE 6.2

Read the review of *Fantastic Mr Fox* and answer the following questions in full sentences.

1. If a performance of *Fantastic Mr Fox* began at 2.30 pm at what time would it end?

2. Who wrote the music for this puppetry version of *Fantastic Mr Fox*?

3. (a) With which other version does Nuala Calvi compare this *Fantastic Mr Fox*?

   (b) What do you learn from her review about the earlier version?

4. What aspect of this production did Nuala Calvi find disappointing?

5. In what ways did the set contribute to her enjoyment of the play?

6. What did she like about the humour?

 Your turn to write

EXERCISE 6.3

1. Invent a terrible beast and write the story of a human's encounter with it.

2. Write a review of any play (or film) that you have seen recently.

3. Retell in your own words any story you already know about humans battling to defeat frightening beasts (such as St George and the Dragon, Daniel in the Lions' Den or Red Riding Hood). Make it as vivid as you can.

4. Write any kind of story which either of the two extracts above suggests to you.

5. Design an advertising leaflet to persuade people to buy tickets for *Fantastic Mr Fox*. Use the information in the review.

6. Do you like reading fantasy books? Write an essay explaining your views. (It doesn't matter whether you are a fantasy fan or a fantasy hater!) Mention books that you have read or seen as films.

✐ Improve your writing

Write an essay on the following question.

> Why do so many children enjoy reading fantasy books?

1. Jot down some very quick reasons in note form, such as:
    - They build on fairy stories
    - They help them escape to other worlds
    - They link with computer games and TV
    - They are often in series
    - Grown-ups often hate them – children like to be different

2. Aim for about five points and arrange in the best order.

3. Think of an interesting opening statement such as 'When I surveyed my class with a questionnaire about their reading preferences, half the girls and three-quarters of the boys chose fantasy as their favourite genre.'

4. Think of a punchy concluding statement which doesn't repeat something you've already said. For example 'As a person who much prefers books about historical fiction to fantasy, I'm fascinated by the obsession for fantasy so many of my classmates have. I begin to understand the reasons but I'm not converted – yet.'

5. Now write your essay in seven paragraphs – introduction, five main points and conclusion.

'Jabberwocky'

This famous 'nonsense' poem was first published in Lewis Carroll's children's novel *Through the Looking-Glass and What Alice Found There* in 1871. The book was a sequel to *Alice's Adventures in Wonderland* (1865).

1   'Twas brillig, and the slithy toves
    Did gyre and gimble in the wabe:
    All mimsy were the borogoves,
    And the mome raths outgrabe.

5   'Beware the Jabberwock, my son!
    The jaws that bite, the claws that catch!
    Beware the Jubjub bird, and shun
    The frumious Bandersnatch!'

    He took his vorpal sword in hand:
10   Long time the manxome foe he sought —
    So rested he by the Tumtum tree,
    And stood a while in thought.

    And, as in uffish thought he stood,
    The Jabberwock, with eyes of flame,
15   Came whiffling through the tulgey wood,
    And burbled as it came!

    One two! One two! And through and through
    The vorpal blade went snicker-snack!
    He left it dead, and with its head
20   He went galumphing back.

    'And hast thou slain the Jabberwock?
    Come to my arms, my beamish boy!
    Oh frabjous day! Callooh! Callay!'
    He chortled in his joy.

25   'Twas brillig, and the slithy toves
    Did gyre and gimble in the wabe:
    All mimsy were the borogoves,
    And the mome raths outgrabe

    Lewis Carroll (1871)

EXERCISE 6.5

Read this poem several times.

1. Now draw – or make a diagram of – the death of the Jabberwock, including as many details from the poem as you can.

2. Label your drawing/diagram with quotations from the poem.

 Discuss

EXERCISE 6.6

1. If this poem is 'nonsense' how do we know it is English nonsense and not in another language? Look at the:
   - words which link the nonsense words
   - shapes of the sentences
   - sound of the nonsense words.

2. How has Lewis Carroll formed his nonsense words? Look carefully at, for example:
   - slithy
   - mimsy.

3. Look at the rhyme scheme in 'Jabberwocky'. It is very regular. Lewis Carroll is using the traditional form of the **ballad** – old poems which told stories and were usually listened to rather than read. Ballads often end by repeating the opening verse as 'Jabberwocky' does. It makes it sound ancient and mysterious.

   Read 'Jabberwocky' aloud and discuss its rhyme and rhythm.

✤ Explore poetry further

Write a nonsense poem of your own.

- Decide what atmosphere you want to create.
- Decide whether it will be a ballad or some other sort of poem.
- Coin some new words by combining two existing words.

Grammar and punctuation

Apostrophes

The apostrophe – that little hanging comma above the line – has two main jobs.

First it stands in for a letter or group of letters which has been left out:

- **Wouldn't** is short for 'would not'.
- **M'chester** (on a sign post) is short for 'Manchester'.
- **O'clock** is short for 'of the clock' which is what people used to say.
- **It's** is short for 'it is' or 'it has'.
- **I'm** is short for 'I am'.

EXERCISE 6.7

1. Link these shortened forms (a–h) with their full versions (i–viii):

(a)	C'bury	(i)	is not
(b)	can't	(ii)	there is
(c)	let's	(iii)	Peterborough
(d)	P'boro	(iv)	who is
(e)	there's	(v)	cannot
(f)	you'll	(vi)	let us
(g)	who's	(vii)	Canterbury
(h)	isn't	(viii)	you will

2. Six apostrophes have been left out of the following passage. Your job is to put them in.

    Abigail knew shed have to hurry. Shed been told to get to the shop before it shut at six oclock. 'Weve run out of salt,' she told Mr Evans, the corner shopkeeper. 'Were having fish and chips for supper and itd be horrible without salt.'

Apostrophes (continued)

The second job of the apostrophe is to show the 'owner' of something. You are almost always safe if you follow this rule: the apostrophe goes after the last letter of whoever or whatever the thing belongs to and is followed by an 's'. For example:

- Owner is singular (only one): The books owned by one girl are the **girl's books**.

- Owner is singular and ends with an '-s' or '-ss': The costume worn by the actress is the **actress's costume**.

- Owner is plural (more than one) and does not end with an '-s': The books owned by 29 men are the **men's books**.

However, if the owner is plural and *does* end with an '-s' then the apostrophe comes after the 's' and no second 's' is needed. For example:

The books owned by 29 boys are the **boys' books**.

Do not get into the habit of scattering apostrophes in your writing every time you use an s!

You have to think quite hard every time. In the following sentence the letter 's' is sometimes connected with an apostrophe and sometimes not:

Sarah's sisters left their **neighbours'** dogs tied to two posts outside ASDA while they went inside to buy two boxes of chocolates for their **aunt's** birthday.

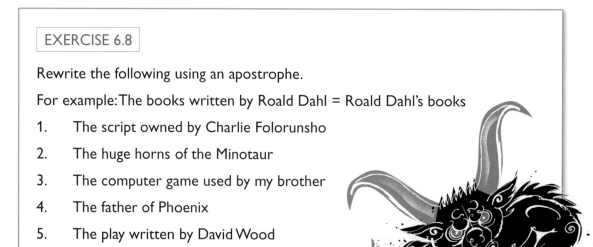

EXERCISE 6.8

Rewrite the following using an apostrophe.

For example: The books written by Roald Dahl = Roald Dahl's books

1. The script owned by Charlie Folorunsho
2. The huge horns of the Minotaur
3. The computer game used by my brother
4. The father of Phoenix
5. The play written by David Wood
6. The big bag of crisps bought for all the boys
7. The coat worn by the princess
8. The sister of the princesses

Adjectives for comparing

An adjective may be compared in three degrees: positive, comparative and superlative:

Positive	Comparative	Superlative
fierce	fiercer	fiercest
pale	paler	palest
tiny	tinier	tiniest
enjoyable	more enjoyable	most enjoyable
frightening	more frightening	most frightening
good	better	best
bad	worse	worst

Most short adjectives take 'er' and 'est', sometimes with a slight change in spelling (such as 'easy – easier – easiest'). Longer adjectives need 'more' or 'most' in front of them. Exceptions such as 'good – better – best' are relatively rare and just have to be learnt.

EXERCISE 6.9

Comparative adjectives activities:

1. Write a list of ten adjectives. Write the comparative and superlative forms next to them.

2. Put the right comparative or superlative adjectives in these sentences:

    (a) The koala is the _____ (sweet) little creature in the world.

    (b) London is _____ (crowded) than Edinburgh.

    (c) *Shadow of the Minotaur* is the _____ (exciting) fantasy I have read.

    (d) The Little Angel is one of London's _____ (small) theatres.

    (e) *Matilda* is the _____ (good) thing Roald Dahl has written.

    (f) This slave girl is pretty, this one is quite attractive but this one over here is by far the _____ (beautiful).

Vocabulary and spelling

1. The Minotaur in the Greek myth was part-man and part-bull. *Taurus* is Latin for a bull. *Tauros* is Ancient Greek for a bull.

   Taurine is an adjective meaning bull-like. So: The gigantic **taurine** head reared over Theseus.

   Taurus, the bull, is the name given to a bull-shaped group of stars.

   Taurus, the bull, is the second sign of the zodiac. Astrologers believe that people born between 20 April and 20 May are influenced by this sign. (Look up and learn the difference between an **astronomer** and an **astrologer**.)

   Tauromachy is another word for bull fighting.

2. **Grandiloquent** means grandly spoken. It comes from the Latin word *loquor* which means 'I speak'.

3. **Muzzle** is spelt with a double z. Learn also:

   guzzle   puzzle   embezzle   sizzle   nuzzle   dazzle   drizzle

4. **Monstrous** is an adjective formed from the noun 'monster' – but, unusually, the adjective has no 'e'. Learn also:

   ● disastrous (from disaster)
   ● wondrous (from wonder)
   ● leprous (from leper)

5. **Historical** is the adjective formed from 'history'. Learn also:

   ● geographical (from geography)
   ● biological (from biology)
   ● philosophical (from philosophy)
   ● geometrical (from geometry)

   Work with a partner and test each other. Remember it is much more important to be able to write a word down correctly than to spell it aloud.

EXERCISE 6.10

Vocabulary activity:

Find out what the following words – all from *loquor* (I speak) – mean and use them in sentences of your own:

1.   eloquent

2.   loquacious

3.   ventriloquist

Speaking and listening

1.   Work in a group of three or four. Prepare a shared reading of the extract from *Shadow of the Minotaur*. Make it as dramatic as you can. Perform your reading to another group.

2.   Organise formal class discussions on (a) 'Are computer games a good thing?' and (b) 'Why do so many children and young people like fantasy?'

3.   Look through some anthologies of poetry. Choose a poem – or part of one – which you like, perhaps with a fantasy theme. Learn it by heart. Perform it for the others in your class.

4.   Work in a pair. Pretend that one of you loves reading and the other hates it. Decide who is to take which point of view – it doesn't matter what you really think. Work out your arguments and see if you can persuade your partner to agree with you.

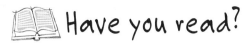 # Have you read?

These books are all fantasies to some extent:

- *Shadow of the Minotaur* by Alan Gibbons (2000)
- *His Dark Materials* (trilogy) by Philip Pullman (1995, 1997, 2000)
- *The Wonderful Wizard of Oz* by Frank L Baum (1900)
- *The Amazing Maurice and his Educated Rodents* by Terry Pratchett (2001)
- *Alice in Wonderland* by Lewis Carroll (1865)
- *The Lion, the Witch and the Wardrobe* by CS Lewis, illustrated by Pauline Baynes (1950)
- *The Witches* by Roald Dahl (1983)
- *The Earthsea Quartet* by Ursula K Le Guin (1993)
- *The Wind Singer* by William Nicholson (2000)
- *Grinny* by Nicholas Fisk (1973)
- *Elidor* by Alan Garner (1965)
- *Mrs Frisby and the Rats of NIMH* by Robert O'Brien (1971)
- *Skellig* by David Almond (1998)
- *The Search for Wondla* by Tony DiTerlizzi (2010)
- *Crystal* by Rebecca Lisle (2010)

✔ And if you've done all that ...

- Take a short story you know and like (it could also be a fairy story, folk tale or myth). Adapt it as a play. You could write out the scripts by hand or word process them on a computer. Get a group of friends to perform your play for the rest of the class.

- Conduct a survey of some children and adults to find out what they think about fantasy and whether they like it or not. Find a way of making your findings clear (e.g. in a graph or table) and display them on a wall poster.

- Is fantasy better in books than in plays and films? Work out your views and the reasons for them. Write a letter to Philip Pullman, who wrote the *His Dark Materials* trilogy, or to JK Rowling, author of the Harry Potter books, or any other writer of a fantasy that you have read, expressing your opinion.

Chapter 7 Dangerous creatures

Shark alert

Mau, who lives somewhere in the tropics, is coping with the many challenges of building a new life and having to be a community leader after losing his village and everyone he knows in a 19th century tsunami. Here he encounters a shark.

1   Things happen or do not happen, thought Mau, and he felt the deep blue
       waters open up under him. The sunlight shone blue through the waves
       above him, but below Mau it was green, shading to black. And there was
       Ataba, hanging in the light, not moving. Blood uncoiled in the water around
5   him like smoke from a slow fire.

       A shadow passed over the sun, and a grey shape slid overhead.

       It was the canoe. As Mau grabbed the priest there was a splash, and Pilu
       swam out of a cloud of bubbles. He pointed frantically.

       Mau turned to see a shark already circling. It was a small grey, although
10   when there is blood in the water then no shark is small, and this one
       seemed to fill the whole of Mau's world.

       He thrust the old man towards Pilu, but kept his attention on the shark,
       looking into its mad, rolling eye as it swam past. He thrashed around a little
       to keep its attention on him and didn't relax until, behind
15   him, he could feel the boat rocking as Ataba was
       hauled up for the second time.

       The shark was going to rush him on the
       next pass, Mau could tell. And – suddenly
       it didn't matter. This was the world, all of
20   it, just this silent blue ball of a soft light,
       and the shark and Mau, without a knife.
       A little ball of space, with no time.

       He swam gently towards the fish, and
       this seemed to worry it.

25   His thoughts came slowly and calmly,
       without fear. Pilu and Ataba would be
       out of the water now, and that was
       what mattered.

30 When a shark is coming at you, you are already dead, old Nawi had said, and since you were already dead, then anything was worth trying …

He rose gently and gulped a lungful of air. When he sank back down again, the shark had turned and was slicing through the water towards him.

Wait … Mau trod water gently as the shark came onward, as grey as Locaha. There would be one chance.

35 More sharks would be here any second, but a second passed slowly in the arena of light.

Here it came …

Wait. Then … *Does not happen*, said Mau to himself, and let all his breath out in a shout.

40 The shark turned as if it had hit a rock, but Mau did not wait for it to come back. He spun in the water and raced for the canoe as fast as he dared, trying to make the maximum of speed with the minimum of splash. As the brothers hauled him aboard, the shark passed underneath them.

'You drove it away!' said Pilu, heaving him up. 'You shouted and it turned and
45 ran!'

Because old Nawi was right, Mau thought. Sharks don't like noise, which sounds louder underwater; it doesn't *matter* what you shout, so long as you shout it loud!

It probably wouldn't have been a good idea if the shark had been really
50 hungry, but it had *worked*. If you were alive, what else mattered?

Should he tell them? Even Milo was looking at him with respect. Without being quite able to put words to it, he felt that being mysterious and a little dangerous was not a bad thing right now.

From *Nation* by Terry Pratchett (2008)

EXERCISE 7.1

Read the extract from *Nation* and answer the following questions in full sentences.

1. Whom did Mau rescue from the shark?

2. What facts do you learn about the shark's near-victim from this passage?

3. What has attracted the shark and what does Mau notice about it?

4. Which words and phrases does Terry Pratchett use to emphasise the things about the shark which frighten Mau most?

5. Who was waiting in the canoe?

6. Whose advice did Mau remember and what was it?

7. What do you learn about Mau's character from this passage?

Snap! Moment a camera-shy shark decided enough was enough

1 This was one camera-shy subject who was clearly in no mood for a close-up.

While a group of photographers photographed tiger sharks in the Bahamas, one of the predators suddenly grabbed one of their cameras in its jaws and swam off.

5 Karin Brussaard from the Netherlands, who captured the commotion on film, said: 'There were about six or seven tiger sharks down there and we couldn't believe our luck.

'We were having a great time photographing them all until one

10 diver swam towards one of them trying to get a better shot.

'The shark suddenly seemed to get angry and snatched the camera right out of his hands.

15 'I couldn't believe it. It swam away with it and we all just looked on in amazement.

'Luckily it did drop it eventually and remarkably the camera

20 seemed only to have a couple of scratches on it.'

From an article published in *The Telegraph* (2010)

EXERCISE 7.2

Look at the photograph and the text on page 89 that appeared in *The Daily Telegraph* and answer the following questions in full sentences.

1. Who took this photograph?

2. Who was in the water?

3. Describe in your own words what happened.

4. What two things particularly surprised the person quoted?

5. What is the purpose of the first sentence in this passage?

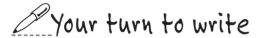 Your turn to write

EXERCISE 7.3

1. Imagine you are Ataba. Retell the story of what happens in the extract from *Nation* from your own point of view. Add as many details from your own imagination as you like.

2. Write a story about a child who has to face dangers and challenges.

3. Write a story about an encounter between a human being and a dangerous wild animal.

4. Read one of the books in the 'Have you read?' section and write a review of it.

5. Find out everything you can about sharks. Write a short article about their habits and behaviour for a wildlife magazine for children your age.

6. Imagine the conversation between Karin Brussaard and the *Daily Telegraph* journalist she spoke to. Write it in the format of a play script.

7. Write a poem about a dangerous but fascinating wild animal.

8. Write about loneliness, challenges, disaster or dangerous wild animals in any way you wish.

Improve your writing

EXERCISE 7.4

1. Use some of the following phrases in a short, colourful descriptive paragraph – or a short poem – about a hot place or day:

steamy grass	dry, dusty path	relentless sun
shrivelled leaves	smiling sunflowers	shady place

2. Now list some phrases of your own relating to cold places. Make them as original as you can.

3. Write a short, colourful descriptive paragraph – or a poem – about a cold place or day using some of your phrases.

'The Maldive Shark'

Herman Melville's most famous work is the novel *Moby Dick* (1851). This poem is also about a large sea hunter.

1 About the Shark, phlegmatical one,
   Pale sot of the Maldive sea,
   The sleek little pilot-fish, azure and slim,
   How alert in attendance be.
5 From his saw-pit of mouth, from his charnel of maw,
   They have nothing of harm to dread,
   But liquidly glide on his ghastly flank
   Or before his Gorgonian head;
   Or lurk in the port of serrated teeth
10 In white triple tiers of glittering gates,
   And there find a haven when peril's abroad,
   An asylum in jaws of the Fates!
   They are friends; and friendly they guide him to prey,
   Yet never partake of the treat—
15 Eyes and brains to the dotard lethargic and dull,
   Pale ravener of horrible meat.

Herman Melville (1888)

EXERCISE 7.5

Read 'The Maldive Shark' and answer the following questions in full sentences.

1. What is the pilot-fish doing?

2. Why does the shark not swallow it?

3. How does the pilot-fish benefit the shark?

4. In what ways is the pilot-fish different from the shark?

5. The first four lines of the poem are a single sentence. What is the subject of the sentence?

6. List the three phrases which come before the subject of the sentence. Then explain what each phrase adds to the meaning of the sentence.

7. Look up and explain the meanings of these words: (a) phlegmatical (line 1), (b) sot (line 2), (c) charnel (line 5), (d) maw (line 5), (e) Gorgonian (like a Gorgon – but who or what was that?) (line 8), (f) dotard (line 15), (g) lethargic (line 15) and (h) ravener (line 16).

 Discuss

EXERCISE 7.6

1. Pick out and comment on all the details – words and phrases – which tell you how fearsome the shark is.

2. Can you work out why it is called a <u>pilot</u>-fish?

3. Is this poem:

    (a) an account of why the poet is frightened of sharks

    (b) a reflection on the tiny pilot-fish's easy relationship with the shark

    (c) a description of a shark

    (d) an appreciation of sharks?

4. Look at the poem's rhyme pattern. Write it out in the usual way, calling the first line A, the second B and so on.

5. What effect does the rhyme have on the poem?

✳ Explore poetry further

1. Write a poem of your own about an unusual relationship between animals or people.

2. Use the internet and poetry anthologies to find other poems about fish.

Grammar and punctuation

Conjunctions

Conjunctions are words such as 'and', 'but', 'although' and 'because' which link other words, sentences and ideas together.

For example:

- Sharks **and** stingrays are common in tropical waters.
- Mau was very frightened of the shark **but** managed to scare it away.
- A shark snatched a camera from a diver **although** the equipment was later retrieved unharmed.
- I wouldn't want to be in the water with sharks **because** I am not a confident swimmer.

Other examples of conjunctions are:

| or | as | if | so | before | until | unless | after |

EXERCISE 7.7

A sentence which contains a single statement (with only one verb) is called a simple sentence. Rewrite these pairs of sentences as one longer sentence using a conjunction. You may need to alter the words slightly.

For example:

- Many people enjoy diving. You can use special underwater cameras.
- Many people enjoy diving **because** you can use special underwater cameras.

1. Sharks live mostly in the tropics. Whales are commoner near the poles.

2. My little sister is hungry. We must have lunch soon.

3. Dolphins are mammals. They swim like fish.

4.   We must hurry to the classroom. We shall be late.

5.   Terry Pratchett has written many novels. Only one, *Nation*, has become a play at the National Theatre.

6.   Tiger sharks are one type of shark. Great whites are another.

7.   Sharks do not usually grab cameras. It was an interesting news item.

8.   Sharks can sense blood in the water. It means food.

Compound sentences

A longer sentence in which two or more sentences are hooked together (such as any of the ones you created for Exercise 7.7) is known as a compound sentence.

You can sometimes move the conjunction around in your sentence to change its shape. It is as if the sentence were being turned inside out.

● Sharks swim towards blood in the water because they need food.

means almost the same as

● Because they need food, sharks swim towards blood in the water.

And:

● Some people enjoy diving to photograph sharks although it is potentially quite a dangerous activity.

means almost the same as:

● Although it is potentially quite a dangerous activity, some people enjoy diving to photograph sharks.

Try occasionally turning a sentence inside out to add variety to your writing.

EXERCISE 7.8

Write six pairs of compound sentences. First write the sentence with the conjunction in the middle. Then turn it back to front and put the conjunction at the beginning of the sentence. For example:

1.   (a)   My grandmother could not join us as she was ill.

(b)   As she was ill, my grandmother could not join us.

2.   (a)   I enjoy sea stories because they remind me of holidays on the coast.

(b)   Because they remind me of holidays on the coast, I love sea stories.

EXERCISE 7.9

Now for some practice to help you revise what we have learnt so far in this book about punctuation.

Write out these sentences adding the correct full stops, commas, hyphens, dashes and apostrophes.

1. Is reading about dangerous animals Melissas favourite activity

2. I am interested in sharks dolphins whales seals sea lions and anything else which is large and aquatic

3. Do you think Karin Brussaard was using a hand held camera

4. Terry Pratchetts books are my fathers favourite reading

5. Help Shark Come quickly

6. Its safest to use a diving bell to observe sharks or else

7. The camera grabbing shark astonished the photograph hungry divers

8. That shark its snatched his camera

Vocabulary and spelling

1. A **predator** is a carnivorous (flesh eating) animal which plunders or takes food violently. It comes from the Latin word *praeda*, which means 'plunder'. We also use the adjectives **predatory** and **predacious** to describe animals, or sometimes people, and their behaviour.

   Predatory pricing, for example, is offering goods for sale at such low prices that it puts competing shops out of business.

2. The word **photograph** comes from the Greek words for light and writing. It literally means 'to write in light'.

   Other words from these roots include **graphology** (study of handwriting), **biography** (writing about a life), **photosynthethis** (process by which plants use light to create oxygen) and **phototherapy** (use of light in treatment of illness).

3. The word **commotion** means a noisy upheaval and comes from the Latin words *cum* (with) and *movere* (to move). We get obvious words such as **move**, **movement** and **motion** from the same root. Less obviously linked, perhaps, are words such as **demotion** which means the movement of someone from a more senior to a more junior position or **emotion**, the outward movement of deep, intense, inner feelings.

4. The word **punctuation** comes from the Latin word for a point. We put points – or full stops – in our sentences to make them clearer or more pointed.

   We get **puncture** from the same Latin root. Something – such as a car tyre – which is punctured has been pricked by a point.

   A **punctual** person is someone who does everything on the dot or the precise point of time.

EXERCISE 7.10

Use these words in sentences of your own:

photographic	lexicography	predatory	emotional
punctilious	punctured	graph	demoted

EXERCISE 7.11

These words all contain 'our':

neighbour	savour	colour	humour	flavour
saviour	favour	honour	labour	glamour

Write each of these words into a phrase (short part-sentence). You can add extra letters such as ''s', 'ed' or 'ing' if you need to. For example: our neighbour's car, coloured pencils, sense of humour. Try to think of several uses for each word. It will give you practice in writing them down correctly spelt.

EXERCISE 7.12

These words all use the letters 'gh' but they do not all sound alike or rhyme:

laugh	dough	plough	thorough	through
cough	daughter	borough	bough	brought

Work with a partner. Look at the words above.

1.   Make sure you both know how to say each word aloud.

2.   Make sure you both know how to write each correctly spelt.

3.   Group the words according to their sounds and add extra words that use 'ough' or 'augh' to each group.

Speaking and listening

1.   Think of an animal which you think is really interesting. You have one minute to convince a partner that it is special. Spend a few minutes working out what you are going to say first. Take it in turns to speak.

2.   Choose a famous person, dead or alive. Find out what you can about him or her. Then pretend that you are that person and give a short talk to the rest of the class about 'yourself'. Ask the class to question you once you have finished.

3.   Work in a group of four. Discuss what you know about natural disasters across the world and their effects – tidal waves, hurricanes, earthquakes, volcanic eruptions, famines, epidemics and so on. What, if anything, can we, or should we, do to help people who are affected?

 Have you read?

All these books feature natural disasters and/or encounters with dangerous wild animals:

- *Running Wild* by Michael Morpurgo (2009)
- *Edge of Nowhere* by John Smelcer (2010)
- *The Blue-eyed Aborigine* by Rosemary Hayes (2010)
- *Floodland* by Marcus Sedgwick (2000)
- *Plague 99* by Jean Ure (1989)
- *Empty World* by John Christopher (1977)
- *The Call of the Wild* by Jack London (1903)
- *Moby Dick* by Herman Melville (1851)

✔ And if you've done all that ...

- Find out what you can about sharks: their biology, habitat, problems they have or create and so on. Focus on facts rather than on 'horror' stories. Use reference books and websites such as www.sharktrust.org. Design a poster for the classroom wall which displays what you think is the most important information.

- Sir Terry Pratchett is one of Britain's most famous writers. Find out what you can about him, his life and work and prepare a short talk about him for the class.

- If you wanted to observe sharks in the wild (as opposed to in a large-scale aquarium) where would/could you go? Research the possibilities carefully and write a short report summarising which destination you would choose or recommend and why.

Chapter 8 Traditional tales

Uba-na-ner the magician

Every culture has its folk, fairy or traditional stories which are passed down from adults to children. You will almost certainly know, for example, Cinderella and Red Riding Hood. Here is a traditional tale from Egypt.

1 Uba-na-ner was a handsome and clever young man whose speciality was magic. And everything seemed to be going his way.

He was a great favourite of King Nebka, the Pharaoh of Egypt, who admired Uba-na-ner's
5 skill as a magician. So the king gave the young man a large and elegant house whose many windows and verandas looked across the great glassy River Nile.

Something else was making Uba-na-ner very
10 happy too. He was engaged to marry a beautiful, young woman with glossy, dark hair and eyes like amber. He was looking forward to bringing her home to his riverside house and raising a family with her there.

15 Then his world fell apart. On the very day that he was to be married his pretty bride ran away with another man!

Uba-na-ner was furious. For several days he shut himself away in his house unable to think straight. He wanted revenge.
20 Eventually he thought of a plan.

The young magician fetched his box made of black ebony wood and held together by finely wrought bands of gold and silver. This was where he kept his copies of some ancient magic spells written on rolled-up papyrus.

After consulting the words on the scroll, Uba-na-ner took a piece of white
25 wax. This he moulded in the warmth of his hands into the shape of a small white crocodile.

He breathed on his model and whispered some magic words. Suddenly the creature began to twitch, and it grew bigger and bigger. Soon it was a

fearsome, thrashing crocodile, huge with a long muzzle and ugly interlocking
30 teeth. But it stayed as white as snow – like the wax it was made from.

'Fetch my enemy!' commanded Uba-na-ner. The gigantic white reptile swam
powerfully away into the waters of the Nile.

Uba-na-ner knew that his former fiancée's husband would, sooner or later,
bathe in the Nile, and so it proved. A few days later the great white
35 crocodile returned to Uba-na-ner with the hapless young man held tightly
in its monstrous jaws.

'Kill him!' Uba-na-ner signalled. The crocodile disappeared back into the
Nile and the young man was never seen alive again.

Clearly it was murder and it wasn't long before King Nebka heard about
40 the young man's disappearance. The bereaved bride went to see the King.
She wept and wept, but she also told him who the
murderer was.

Nebka was very upset. He liked Uba-na-ner
and found it hard to believe that his
45 favourite would do such a thing.
Nevertheless he had to
question the young
magician.

Uba-na-ner
50 denied nothing.
Instead he led
Nebka to the
bank of the
Nile and
55 clapped his
hands. The
white crocodile
reappeared at
his summons,
60 the dead man's
body still in its
mouth.

The King's
attendants

65 were very frightened. Never had they seen a Nile crocodile so colossal or so ruthless. But Nebka was calm and brave. And something about the king's tranquil courage made Uba-na-ner – at last – realise what a terrible thing he had done.

Regretting his action and feeling real remorse for the distress he had
70 caused, Uba-na-ner made a quick movement with his hands. He said something which no one else understood. Instantly the big, muscular crocodile began to shrink. It stopped moving. Soon, as they watched, it had turned back into a small, white, wax figure.

In his house, Uba-na-ner went to the black, gold and silver casket and put
75 the wax model safely inside with the papyrus scroll of magic spells.

Then he went to King Nebka, knelt before him and offered him the box, because he was truly sorry for what he had done.

'I think you really do regret your evil deed,' said the Pharaoh, 'so I will pardon you and you can remain one of my courtiers. However, you will
80 never be allowed to have this box again. It will remain hidden for ever in my palace.'

Traditional Egyptian tale, retold by Susan Elkin

EXERCISE 8.1

Read the traditional Egyptian tale above and answer the following questions in full sentences.

1. Where, exactly, did Uba-na-ner keep the instructions for his spells?

2. What did Uba-na-ner find attractive about the Pharaoh's daughter?

3. What crime was Uba-na-ner guilty of?

4. Give another word or group of words for (a) revenge (line 19),
(b) bereaved (line 40), (c) summons (line 59) and (d) remorse (line 69).

5. Describe the crocodile in your own words.

6. Explain in your own words why Uba-na-ner was so upset on what would have been his wedding day.

7. Why did King Nebka show mercy to Uba-na-ner?

A traditional Egyptian recipe

Falafel is a traditional Egyptian food. It looks like tiny burgers but contains no meat. It is made from chickpeas (or other sorts of peas, beans or lentils) with spices. Office workers in Cairo buy freshly cooked falafel in rolls from kiosks and take-away shops at lunchtime. Here is a recipe (do not try to make falafel yourself without adult help):

1   1 large tin of chickpeas or lentils

           1 large onion, chopped into pieces

           1 teaspoonful ground coriander

           1 teaspoonful ground cumin

5   1 clove of garlic, peeled and crushed (in a garlic press)

           A little salt and pepper (if you like it)

           A handful of wholemeal flour to dip the falafel in before cooking

           Vegetable oil for frying

Wash your hands. Get out all the ingredients.

10   Drain the chickpeas or lentils. Put all the ingredients except the flour and oil into a food processor or blender. Switch on and process until fairly smooth. Tip or scrape mixture into a bowl.

Take a tablespoonful of the mixture in your

15   (clean) hands. Roll it into a small flat cake. Dip the falafel in the flour and put it on a large plate. Do this until all the mixture is

20   used up.

Heat the oil in a frying pan. Fry the falafel gently until brown on both sides. Unless you have a very

25   large frying pan, you will probably need to cook the falafel in batches.

Falafel is tasty in rolls, baps or pitta bread; or try it with salad.

EXERCISE 8.2

Read the traditional Egyptian recipe and answer the following questions in full sentences.

1. Which two spices are used in falafel?

2. Explain in your own words why you will probably not be able to cook your falafel all at once.

3. Would you offer falafel to a vegetarian guest and, if so, why?

4. Where can you see falafel being eaten today?

5. You should always wash your hands before cooking but why is it particularly important when you are making falafel?

6. How can you tell that your falafel is cooked?

✎ Your turn to write

EXERCISE 8.3

1. Write a story about a crocodile or a magician (or both).

2. Make up a story about anything you wish with the title 'Revenge' or 'Remorse'.

3. Write a recipe for any food you know how to cook and like eating. Include an introduction like the one to the falafel recipe.

4. Uba-na-ner's fiancée broke her promise to him because she fell in love with the man killed on Uba-na-ner's orders. Imagine you are her and write her story. You could write in the form of a diary.

5. Write in any way you choose about Egypt.

6. Write a description of a river you know.

7. Write a review of a book which you have read.

✐ Improve your writing

EXERCISE 8.4

Traditional – or fairy – stories often:

- begin 'Once upon a time …'
- end 'And they lived happily ever after.'
- use short sentences
- feature people in simple jobs such as woodcutters
- are about kings, queens, princes and princesses
- show poor people being lucky
- show wicked people being punished
- end with a marriage
- are quite short.

Write a fairy story of your own for a young child to read. If you bring in as many of the nine elements listed above your work will have an authentic fairy tale 'feel'.

'Retelling of a Chinese Folk Tale'

Jason Meres was 21 when he wrote this poem. He lives in Colorado, USA.

1   The sunlight falls softly amongst the thick-limbed trees,
     A woman, weeping softly on her knees.
     As one must fall the other must arise,
     And in so doing,
5   The first be spared demise.
     The task of which, ne'er easy, and ne'er light.
     The fires of swift revenge, this girl will soon ignite.

     Her eyes, the sparkling jewels, the legends of great kings remained.
     Though, in silence, the subtle twinge of pain.
10   Regret, in form and balanced to her plight,
     She sees her quarry, the truth is brought to light.

One shot, the trees stir, birds take to wing,
And with the fall of memory, the axemen's fatal swing.

A footstep, to knees she falls,
15   The weight of her harsh deed enthrals her heart.
Shadow moves the sundial to its mark,
Paralysed in memory the daughter, the friend, the lover.
And how she was loved.
Moonlit hair glistens and shimmers.
20   Vengeance wrought, and duty done.
The final era of love, the final act of selflessness.
One shot. Love is gone.

Jason Meres (2005)

EXERCISE 8.5

Read the poem carefully several times.

Write a prose version of this story. Invent as many details as you wish or need, but use as much of the information which is in the poem as you can. Use everything you know about traditional tales to make your story sound like one. Think carefully about your opening sentence, for example.

 Discuss

---

EXERCISE 8.6

1. What do you find interesting about this poem?

2. The poem's title tells us that it is a version in verse of a traditional Chinese story which is why it is included in this chapter. What aspects of the poem remind you of, or are similar to, other traditional tales you know?

3. The phrases 'thick-limbed' and 'glistens and shimmers' are examples of assonance. 'Thick' and 'limbed' do not rhyme or begin with the same sound. Instead they have a matching central vowel sound 'i' which links them. 'Glistened' and 'shimmers' are matched in the same way – also with an 'i' sound.

   Assonance is a common poetic device, often combined with rhyme and alliteration (words which have the same letter or sound in them, usually at the beginning of the word).

   What do you think Jason Meres's use of assonance adds to the meaning of the poem?

4. The poem is set in a forest in daylight. The sun is shining on the sundial. So why is her hair 'moonlit' in the last verse?

 Explore poetry further

Think of any traditional tale you know well and retell it in the form of a poem. Try to bring out imaginative details. For example if you retell the Three Little Pigs, think about their terrible fear when the wolf is terrorising them or if you retell the Princess and the Frog, imagine how she would have felt having to kiss a frog. If you can't think of a suitable story try making a poem from the traditional Egyptian tale at the beginning of this chapter. Make use of assonance if you can.

Grammar and punctuation

Subjects and objects

The subject of a sentence is the person or thing which is 'doing the verb'. The object of a sentence is the person or thing which is affected by the action of the verb. In the following examples, the object is shown in bold:

- Uba-na-ner fetched his **box**.
- Wash your **hands**.
- Office workers buy **falafel**.
- He wanted **revenge**.

EXERCISE 8.7

Copy these sentences. Put a rectangle round the subjects and an oval round the objects:

1. A traditional tale affects many readers.

2. Falafel makes fingers sticky.

3. Uba-na-ner watched the big crocodile.

4. King Nebka forgave Uba-na-ner.

5. Nicola ate her falafel.

The passive voice

You can often reverse the subject and object in a sentence by adjusting the words and using 'by'. If the verb is in the **active** voice, the subject of the sentence 'does' the verb to the object. If the verb is in the **passive** voice, the action of the verb is 'done' to the subject **by** someone or something.

For example:

- The king **rules** his country (active voice).
- The country **is ruled by** its king (passive voice).

EXERCISE 8.8

1. Rewrite the five sentences in Exercise 8.7 in the passive voice.

2. Practise writing sentences in the active and passive. Begin with these words:

    (a) Uba-na-ner's fiancée …

    (b) My cooking …

    (c) Take-away shops in Cairo …

    (d) Falafel …

    (e) A piece of white wax …

    (f) The magician …

    (g) Crocodiles …

    (h) Egyptians …

3. Provide subjects for these objects to form sentences. You will need a verb as well.

(a) … the story.

(b) … the River Nile.

(c) … bad behaviour.

(d) … the smell of falafel frying.

(e) … Uba-na-ner.

(f) … magic spells.

Colons

The colon (:) means 'as follows' or 'like this'. It is useful when you want to introduce a list or some information in your writing. (Sometimes it is used to introduce what someone says, too, as in this example – 'King Nebka said: "I will forgive you."')
For example:

• Here are some examples of traditional stories: Rumpelstiltskin, Alibaba and the Forty Thieves, The Three Little Pigs and Brer Rabbit.

• You make falafel like this: mix up the ingredients, form cakes and fry them.

EXERCISE 8.9

1. Write three sentences including lists in which the list is preceded by a colon. Your sentences can be about anything you like.

2. Make up three sentences containing the words 'like this', 'as follows', 'thus', 'in the following way' or 'for example'. Use a colon to link the next part of the sentence.

(Did you know that Colon is also a town in Panama, in central America and that the colon is part of the digestive system of all mammals?)

Vocabulary and spelling

1. If you are **engaged** to someone, it means that you have agreed to marry him or her. English often has several words which mean almost the same thing. 'Betrothed', 'affianced', 'tokened', 'promised' and 'plighted' all mean the same as 'engaged', although some of these are rather old-fashioned words which you will probably see only in books written long ago.

    Words which are similar in meaning are called 'synonyms'.

    How many synonyms can you think of, or find in a thesaurus*, for (a) colossal, (b) frightened and (c) meal?

    *A thesaurus is a special sort of dictionary which lists groups of synonyms. You can access a dictionary or thesaurus via the internet as well as by using books.

2. **Ruthless** means without mercy or pity. 'Ruth' is an old English word which means mercy. It is now very rarely used other than as part of the word 'ruthless' and in the female name Ruth. Words which have died out – or almost died out – are called 'archaisms'.

    Do you know, or can you find out, what the following female names mean? They are all archaisms, or unusual words in English:

Grace	Prudence	Felicity	Verity
Charity	Sally	Mavis	Flora

3. Many words in English end in '-ss' including the ones ending -ness which we looked at in Chapter 5.

    Some nouns and verbs such as 'distress', 'address' and 'success' use the double 's' for emphasis because the second half of the word is accented. Practise saying these and think of other examples.

    When a noun ending in '-ss' becomes plural, or the word is a part of the verb which needs 's', it takes 'es'. So: distresses, addresses and successes.

    Some nouns such as 'princess', 'actress' and 'mayoress' end in '-ess' because they are the feminine form of other words such as 'prince', 'actor' and 'mayor'. How many other examples can you think of? Be careful with these. They too need 'es' when they are plural and ''s' when they are possessive. So: three actresses, the mayoress's son.

    Then there are adjectives which end in -less such as 'ruthless', 'harmless' and 'careless'. They take 'ly' when they become adverbs. So: ruthlessly, harmlessly and carelessly.

Learn the spelling of these:

confess	discuss	countess's (daughter)	useless
depress	endless	expresses	possesses
progress	(six) princesses	princess's (shoe)	tirelessly
hopeless	effortlessly	needless	wireless
compresses	goddesses	lioness's (tail)	success

Speaking and listening

1. Work with a partner on a traditional story which you both know well (or choose one from one of the books in the 'Have you read?' section). Practise telling it together, taking turns to speak in order to make your version of it as dramatic and interesting as you can. Perform your story for the rest of the class.

2. Working in a group, play 'Pass the Story'. One of you begins a story. After one or two sentences the first person stops, possibly mid-sentence. The next person in the group continues the story and then in turn passes it on. You can also play 'Pass the Story' by saying just one word each and seeing how the story develops.

3. Prepare a short talk about your favourite food or recipe. Give your talk in front of a group or class.

4. In groups, talk about animals in stories. Why are some animals always bad and some always good? Think of examples. Are those animals really like that in nature? Do you like to read about animals in stories? Why, or why not?

5. Interview someone who has been to Egypt. Write an article based on your interview for the school or class magazine.

 Have you read?

These books contain a wide range of traditional stories from all over the world:

*   *The Old Stories: Folk Tales from East Anglia and the Fen Country* by Kevin Crossley-Holland (1997)
*   *Why the Fish Laughed and Other Tales* by Kevin Crossley-Holland (1998)
*   *Tales of Ancient Persia* by Barbara Leonie Picard (1972)

- *Hero Tales From the British Isles* by Barbara Leonie Picard (1963)
- *Folk Tales for Reading and Telling* by Leila Berg (1966)
- *English Fairy Tales* edited by Flora Annie Steel and illustrated by Arthur Rackham (1918)
- *The Adventures of Robin Hood* by Roger Lancelyn Green (1956)
- *Tales of Ancient Egypt* by Roger Lancelyn Green (1967)
- *Hans Andersen's Fairy Tales* (1981)
- *Jamil's Clever Cat: A Bengali Folk Tale* by Fiona French (1998)
- *Mariana and the Merchild: A Folk Tale from Chile* by Caroline Pitcher (2000)
- *The Boy Who Drew Cats and Other Japanese Fairy Tales* by L Hearn (1963)
- *Stories from Around the World* by H Amery (2000)

✔ And if you've done all that ...

- Collect traditional recipes from around the world. Use the internet, cookery books or ask people you know. Create a global cookery booklet. Ideally, you should try out the recipes. You may find you have to edit or rewrite some of them to make the meaning clear. It may also be necessary to suggest slightly different ingredients if the recipe includes items which you cannot buy easily in Britain. Can you sell your booklet to raise money for one of the charities which helps starving people in poor countries?

- Make a large map of Egypt as a poster for the classroom. Show the River Nile and all the major cities. What other information can you get onto it?

- Prepare a short talk for the class about the Ancient Egyptians. Include how they lived, what they believed and what they did. Use a computer program such as PowerPoint to illustrate your talk.

- Find out about the Suez Canal. Where is it, why was it built, by whom and why is (or was) it important?

Chapter 9 Dealing with disability

Crutches

Alan Marshall, who grew up in Queensland, Australia, caught polio in 1908 when he was six. The disease left him permanently paralysed in the legs – especially his right leg – and unable to walk without crutches. He died in 1984.

1   My crutches were gradually becoming part of me. I had developed arms out of proportion to the rest of my body and my armpits were now tough and hard. The crutches did not chafe me any more and I could walk without discomfort.

5   I practised different walking styles, calling them by the names applied to the gaits of horses. I could trot, pace, canter and gallop. I fell frequently and heavily but learned to throw myself into positions that saved my bad leg from injury. I typed the falls I had and when beginning to fall always knew whether

10 it would be a 'bad' or a 'good' fall. If both crutches slipped backwards when I was well advanced on my forward swing I fell backwards and

15 this was the worst fall of all since it often resulted in my being winded or twisting my bad leg beneath me. It was a

20 painful fall and I used to thump the earth with my hands to keep from crying out when I fell in this manner. When

25 only one crutch slipped or stuck a stone or root, I fell forward on to my hands and was never hurt.

    I was never free of bruises or
30 lumps or gravel rashes and every

evening found me attending to some injury I had received that day.

But they did not distress me. I accepted these inconveniences as being part of normal living and I never for a moment regarded them as a result of being crippled, a state which, at this period, I never applied to myself.

35 I began walking to school and became acquainted with exhaustion – the state so familiar to cripples and their constant concern.

I always cut corners, always made in as straight a line as I could to go where I wanted to go. I would walk through clumps of thistles rather than go round them and climb through fences rather than deviate a few yards to go 40 through a gate.

Joe Carmichael and I hunted rabbits and hares together. We went tramping through the bush and across open paddocks with a pack of dogs. When we roused the hare and the dogs gave chase I watched with keen pleasure the kangaroo dog's undulating run, his lowered head close to the ground, the 45 magnificent curve of his neck and shoulders and the swinging, leaning turn of him as he came round after the dodging hare.

After tea, before it was time to go to bed, in that first expectant darkness when the frogs from the swamp began their chirping and the early possums peered out from hollows, I would stand at the gate. In my imagination I 50 would launch myself into a powerful run through the night like an animal. As a dog racing through the night, I experienced no effort, no fatigue and no painful falls.

But I didn't resent my crutches. I could not feel that way. I left them behind in my dreams but I returned to them without resentment.

Slightly adapted from *I Can Jump Puddles* by Alan Marshall (1955)

EXERCISE 9.1

Read the extract from *I Can Jump Puddles* and answer the following questions in full sentences.

1. Why were some falls more serious than others?

2. Why do you think Alan Marshall describes the hunting dog's movements in such detail?

3. How can you tell that Alan Marshall does not feel sorry for himself?

4.   Give another word or short phrase for (a) chafe (line 3), (b) deviate (line 39), (c) undulating (line 44) and (d) expectant (line 47).

5.   List all the details which tell you that the setting for this story is Australia.

6.   Explain what Alan Marshall means by 'I always cut corners' (line 37). Why do you think he did this?

Bones and muscles

1   Your skeleton is a scaffolding of more than 200 living bones. It supports you and keeps you upright. The skeleton may seem fragile, but it carries the whole weight of the body. Your muscles are attached to the bony scaffolding. They pull on the bones to make you move.

5   The word skeleton comes from a Greek word meaning 'dried up', but bones are not dry and brittle. Bones are alive. They grow as we do, repair themselves if they are broken and

10   become stronger as we exercise. A living bone has layers of hard calcium phosphate on the outside and a honeycomb of hard bone and living cells within. This makes it strong and

15   light.

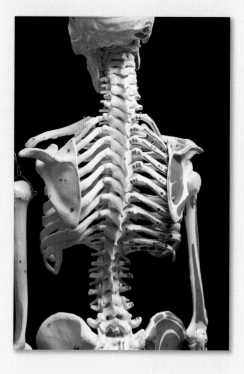

Most organs of the body are soft and delicate. Our bones protect these soft organs from injury. The skull bones, for example, fit tightly together to form a

20   tough case for the brain. The ribs form a rigid case around the lungs and heart and the hip bones enclose the bladder and intestines.

The longest bone in your body is your thigh bone (femur). Your smallest

25   bone is in your ear. It is about the size of a grain of rice.

From *The Young Oxford Encyclopaedia of Science* by Richard Dawkins (2001)

EXERCISE 9.2

Read the passage about bones and muscles and answer the following questions in full sentences.

1. Give another word for (a) scaffolding (line 1), (b) rigid (line 21) and (c) femur (line 24).

2. What are the skeleton's three main jobs?

3. Explain in your own words why the name 'skeleton' (line 5) is inappropriate.

4. Which substance gives bones their strength?

5. How many bones (roughly) do all the pupils in your class have amongst them?

 Your turn to write

EXERCISE 9.3

1. Write a letter to a newspaper or magazine arguing for better facilities for disabled people.

2. Write about skeletons in any way you wish.

3. Imagine that you are unable to walk. Write a story about your life.

4. Write a story about someone who is without one of the senses (sight, hearing, smell, taste or touch) and who then has an operation which gives him or her that sense.

5. Take the title 'Walk'. Write a story, a personal account, a description, your thoughts and feelings or anything else which the title suggests to you.

6. Write about a disabled person that you know. He or she could be blind, deaf, a wheelchair user or have any other sort of disability.

✎ Improve your writing

EXERCISE 9.4

Take great care with language when you are writing about disability. People with disabilities and special needs are entitled to be described with respect and courtesy. Attitudes to this have changed a great deal in recent years.

For example, someone who could not walk or had a limp used to be called a 'cripple'. Alan Marshall uses it in the extract from *I Can Jump Puddles*. The word is used in the best-known translation into English of the Bible which was published in 1611. Many of our cities, including London once had a 'cripple gate' through which disabled people could enter and leave. The word is no longer acceptable.

Words and phrases such as:

- learning difficulty
- visual impairment
- impairment

- wheelchair user
- hearing loss
- access

are considered polite and acceptable.

Write a paragraph commenting on how easy or difficult it is for a disabled person to visit/use your school or another building you know well. Make sure you use polite vocabulary, even though you may find it makes your writing a bit wordy.

But please do not, as most people do, refer to 'disabled toilets'! They would be most unhelpful if you needed to use them …

'Tich Miller'

Wendy Cope worked for 15 years as a primary school teacher before becoming a full-time writer. Her poems are often humorous but also poignant.

```
1      Tich Miller wore glasses with elastoplast-pink frames
       and had one foot three sizes larger than the other.
       When they picked teams for outdoor games
       she and I were always the last two
5      left standing by the wire-mesh fence.
```

We avoided one another's eyes stooping,
perhaps, to re-tie a shoelace, or affecting interest in the flight
of some fortunate bird, and pretended not to hear the urgent conference:
'Have Tubby!' 'No, no, have Tich!'

10   Usually they chose me, the lesser dud,
and she lolloped,
unselected, to the back of the other team.

At eleven we went to different schools.
In time I learned to get my own back,
15   sneering at hockey-players who couldn't spell.

Tich died when she was twelve.

Wendy Cope (1986)

EXERCISE 9.5

Write the questions to which these are the answers:

1. Tich has a club foot which makes her 'lollop' and she wears glasses. These are probably just symptoms of something more serious.

2. Tich and Tubby were always left unpicked for team games until last.

3. The two girls pretend they cannot hear what the other girls are saying.

4. She teases hockey players about their poor spelling.

5. The underlying message of this poem is that life can be cruel but if you are strong and lucky enough to survive you can often find ways of asserting yourself.

 ## Discuss

EXERCISE 9.6

1. The word 'elastoplast' associates Tich with ill-health through the mention of sticking plaster used when something hurts or is bleeding. It also suggests poverty because pink-framed glasses for children used to be the cheapest.

   Are there any other words in the poem which carry several meanings – or connotations, as we usually call them when we're discussing poetry?

2. Wendy Cope has used blank (unrhymed) quite fluid verse in this poem although there are occasional rhymes such as 'games' and 'frames'. How much do you like this poem and why? What effect does the loose form have on your reaction to the poem?

3. The last line consists of six blunt, single-syllable words (known as monosyllables). Is the last line effective? Could the information it contains have been communicated in any other way? Would that have made it a better or a worse poem?

Explore poetry further

'Tich Miller' comes from a slim volume of poetry by Wendy Cope called *Making Cocoa for Kingsley Amis*. It was published by Faber and Faber in 1986. If you have access to a copy read some of the other poems in the book. Alternatively, look for Cope's work in anthologies or on the internet.

Rehearse a reading of 'Tich Miller' (or learn it by heart) and perform it to the class.

Grammar and punctuation

Pronouns

A pronoun is a word which takes the place of a noun. There are several types, and we begin with **personal pronouns**. These are:

	Singular	Plural
1st person	I	we
2nd person	you	you
3rd person	he, she, it	they

For example:

- My dog is called Sheba and he likes bones. ('He' is a pronoun used instead of 'dog' or 'Sheba'.)
- I like apple pie and it is best with custard. ('It' is used instead of repeating 'apple pie'.)
- All the children in my class are excited about the trip to Windsor because they are all looking forward to seeing the castle. ('They' means 'all the children in my class'.)

Possessive pronouns tell you who or what something belongs to:

	Singular	Plural
1st person	my	our
2nd person	your	your
3rd person	his, her, its	their

For example:

- my coat
- his book
- their car
- our mother.

Notice also these forms:

	Singular	Plural
1st person	mine	ours
2nd person	yours	yours
3rd person	his, hers, its	theirs

For example:

- That pen is mine. ('Mine' means 'my pen'.)
- That house is theirs. ('Theirs' means 'their house'.)

Possessive pronouns *never* need an apostrophe. So remember that:

- **Its** means belonging to it.
- **It's** means 'it is' or 'it has'. The apostrophe stands for the missing letters.

Note that many teachers, particularly Latin teachers, may choose to describe these as possessive adjectives, rather than possessive pronouns. This is because in Latin the words my, your, our, etc. are indeed adjectives (*meus, tuus, noster*, etc.). But these English words are indeed pronouns, being the old genitive forms of the corresponding personal pronouns (my = of me, your = of you, etc.); in exactly the same way that the Latin for his/her/its (*eius*) is not an adjective, but is, rather, the genitive form of the pronoun *is, ea, id*.

EXERCISE 9.7

Rewrite these sentences using pronouns to avoid repeating the nouns:

1. The children protested when the children were told off.

2. Emma's father asked Emma to help Emma's disabled brother.

3. The headmaster asked the teachers to come to the headmaster's office when the teachers had dismissed the teachers' classes.

4. The mayoress said that the mayoress had a severe headache.

5. The blind man said that the blind man used a guide dog.

6. Raj took one look at the calculator and saw that it was Raj's.

EXERCISE 9.8

Shorten these sentences by using a possessive pronoun. For example:

- Original sentence: This cat belongs to us. (5 words)
- Rewritten sentence: This cat is ours. (4 words)

1. The new caravan is their property.

2. Does the red scarf belong to her?

3. This wheelchair belongs to me.

4. You must take the responsibility.

5. This is the home which we own.

EXERCISE 9.9

Put **its** or **it's** in the gaps in the following sentences:

1. _____ a pity that _____ raining today.

2. The skeleton in the science lab has lost _____ labels.

3. What a long day _____ been.

4. _____ necessary to visit a museum to find out about _____ history.

5. Ask anyone in the school to tell you about _____ rules.

Pronouns in the accusative

Very few words in English change their form depending on the part that they are playing in a sentence; but pronouns do. Take care, for example, with the pronouns 'me' and 'I', especially in sentences where they are used with another noun or pronoun.

Here are all the personal pronouns again, this time in the accusative case, which we use when they are the object of the sentence or after a preposition:

	Singular	**Plural**
1st person	me	us
2nd person	you	you
3rd person	him, her, it	them

For example:

- He and I are going to play cricket. (Use 'he' and 'I' because you would say 'He is going to play cricket' and 'I am going to play cricket'.)

- Mr Baker gave him and me a detention. (Use 'him' and 'me' because you would say 'Mr Baker gave him a detention' and 'Mr Baker gave me a detention'.)

- He is going to play with you and me. (Use 'you' and 'me' after the preposition 'with'.)

EXERCISE 9.10

Put pronouns in these sentences:

1. Perry and _____ are going to learn the names of all the bones in the body.

2. Jasmine, who is profoundly deaf, invited Ella and _____ to her party.

3. There was trouble ahead for Guy and _____.

4. Uncle John sent presents for James and _____.

5. Clearly Felix and _____ were in trouble because he had lost his crutches.

6. Mrs Burns grumbled at Jake and _____ for being late.

Inverted commas

Inverted commas (" " or ' ') are used to separate the words that someone is speaking from other words in a piece of writing. They are sometimes called speech marks or quotation marks. They always come in pairs at the beginning and end of the words spoken.

They can be single or double. For printed text, the normal convention is to use single inverted commas, unless there is a need to open inverted commas inside a passage that is already in inverted commas, in which case that passage goes in double inverted commas (but you may find it the other way round).

For example:

- 'Peter,' I asked, 'how many times have I said "No" to you today?'

or:

- "Peter," I asked, "how many times have I said 'No' to you today?"

EXERCISE 9.11

Put inverted commas in the correct places in these sentences:

1. Is it morning already? asked Joshua, sitting up in bed.
2. Oh please let me go, pleaded Peter.
3. Dad announced: As soon as Mrs Methuen says Hello I shall be going out.
4. Do you know, said Jack, that the collar bone is called the clavicle?
5. My address, said Mr Micawber, is Windsor Terrace, City Road.

The exact words that someone speaks, enclosed in inverted commas, is known as **direct speech**.

Vocabulary

Words which are opposite in meaning are called **antonyms**.

So, 'weak' is an antonym for 'strong', 'backward' for 'forward' and 'curved' for 'straight'.

Sometimes you can think of several antonyms for one word, particularly if that word has more than one meaning.

For example: antonyms for 'deep' could include 'shallow', 'insincere', 'straightforward', 'light' and 'thin' because the adjective 'deep' has a number of different meanings.

EXERCISE 9.12

How many antonyms can you think of for the following adjectives?

1. simple
2. easy
3. sad
4. bright
5. dark
6. funny

A thesaurus might help you with this.

Spelling

1. In the extract from *I Can Jump Puddles* on page 112, Alan Marshall uses the word 'frequently' (line 6). Check that you know the meanings and spellings of the following words which include 'qu':

eloquent	query	quizzical	quadruped
acquiesce	aquatic	equine	sequence
quartz	antique		

2. In words which come from Ancient Greek the 'f' sound is often written as 'ph' – as in the word 'phosphate' – which is a particularly good example as it has 'ph' twice. Check that you know the meanings and spellings of the following words which include a 'ph':

typhoon	symphony	physical	xylophone
emphasise	triumphant	prophet	catastrophe
philosopher	sphinx		

Speaking and listening

1. Tell the class about any disabled person you know. He or she might be a member of your family, a friend or someone in your community. The person could be blind, deaf, have walking difficulties or have any other sort of disability.

Wheelchair Tennis

2. Work in pairs. Talk about how suitable your school is for people – pupils and adults – with various sorts of disability. Make a list of possible improvements. Put all the lists on a notice board and use them as the basis of a class discussion. You can use the paragraph you wrote about your school in Exercise 9.4 (page 116) as a starting point.

3. Prepare a short talk for the class about the work of one of the charities which works with disabled people – Guide Dogs, Scope or Mencap for example, but there are many other possibilities.

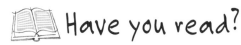 ## Have you read?

These books are by, or partly about, people who have overcome disabilities. Some are fictional and some are autobiographical – factual accounts of people's experiences.

- *I Can Jump Puddles* by Alan Marshall (1955)
- *Good Vibrations: My Biography* Evelyn Glennie (1990)
- *My Left Foot* by Christy Brown (1954)
- *Emma and I* by Sheila Hocken (1977)
- *The Curious Incident Of The Dog in the Night-Time* by Mark Haddon (2003)
- *Flowers for Algernon* by Daniel Keyes (1966)
- *The Illustrated Mum* by Jacqueline Wilson (1999)

✔ And if you've done all that ...

- Read some of the books in the 'Have you read?' section. Write reviews of them. Focus on what you have learnt about the disability in question.

- Design a classroom which would meet the needs of as many different sorts of disabled pupil as possible. Use a computer or sketch your design by hand. It will probably need some notes of explanation. Display your work.

- Get permission from your teacher to contact a disabled person by letter, email or telephone, according to what is appropriate and/or practicable for him or her to use. See if you can invite him or her to school to talk to pupils about his or her experiences.

- Find out the names of as many bones in the body as possible. Create a comic poem or song using as many of these words as you can.

Chapter 10 Sports

A football story

Billy, the central character in this story, is over 80 and is reliving his memories of being a Chelsea Football Club player before the beginning of the Second World War.

1   The first match I ever played for Chelsea Reserves was against Arsenal
     Reserves. There weren't many to watch but Mum came and Joe and Emmy
     and Ossie and they saw me score two goals. One was a simple enough tap-
     in. The other I really enjoyed: a dribble in towards goal, slipping the ball
5   through the legs of one defender, round another and a little chip over the
     goalie. I can still see the look on his face as the ball floated over his head
     and into the goal – horror, disbelief, despair all in one. Lovely!

     I was in the newspapers the
     following day: 'Billy
10   the Kid bamboozles
     the Arsenal.' For the
     whole of the next
     year I was a regular in
     the Chelsea Reserves,
15   and a regular in the
     newspapers too. I didn't think
     life could get any better. But it
     did – for a while at least.

     1939 began as the best
20   year of my life.
     Towards the end of
     that football season I
     was picked for the
     first team. 12th
25   March 1939, just a
     month or so before
     my nineteenth
     birthday, I trotted
     out in my
30   Chelsea shirt for
     the first time.

I was on cloud nine, seventh heaven. We were playing Preston North End away, and we lost badly. No one was looking at me, that was for sure. I was awful, leaden-legged and useless. Ossie, who came to all my matches, took

35 me on one side afterwards and said I had to forget the shirt, forget who I was playing for, where I was playing, all that, and just play the game.

When we played Sunderland the next week at home, it was like I was in the playground again at school, or out in the park with Joe. I ran rings round them, laid on a couple of goals and scored one myself. That was the first

40 time I heard the crowd at the Shed End chanting my name – 'Billy, Billy the Kid! Billy, Billy the Kid!' It sends warm tingles up my spine even now just to think of it. Before the season ended three weeks later I had scored seven more goals and all the papers were saying I'd be playing for England before the end of the year. One paper called me 'Billy the Wonder Kid'. Another

45 said I was as good as Stanley Matthews, maybe better. It would have gone to my head a lot worse if it hadn't been for Ossie.

'Don't read all that stuff, Billy,' he told me. 'Don't even look at it. Not good for you. Let your mum cut it out and stick it in a scrapbook. You can read it later when you're older – can't hurt you then.'

50 Mum did put it all in a scrapbook – she was always taking it out and looking at it and showing it – but it disappeared like everything else.

That summer, Mum married again, married Ossie – and I never even saw it coming. Joe and I were both 'best men' and Emmy was the bridesmaid. So the man who had taught me most of my football, who had been like a father

55 to me since Dad died and a real friend to the family, became my second father. It was a great day for all of us, confetti everywhere and a huge wedding cake made like a football pitch in Chelsea-blue icing. And then they went off to Broadstairs for a week's honeymoon.

They were still away on the third of September when war was declared –

60 another thing I hadn't seen coming. I'd been too busy with my football to worry about what was going on in the world outside.

From *Billy the Kid* by Michael Morpurgo (2000)

EXERCISE 10.1

Read the extract from *Billy the Kid* and answer the following questions in full sentences.

1. What were the approximate dates of (a) Billy's nineteenth birthday and (b) his mother's wedding?

2. Explain in as much detail as you can who you think Ossie is.

3. Why did Ossie tell Billy not to read newspaper accounts of his matches?

4. Why did Billy need to 'forget the shirt' (line 35)?

5. How did Billy feel when he scored his first two goals against Arsenal Reserves?

6. What colour was a Chelsea shirt at this time?

7. How can you tell from this passage that Billy didn't go on being as happy as this?

Running all the way to a gold medal

1 She was a little girl with a future. But when she was born in Kent in 1970, no one imagined that baby Kelly Holmes would one day be a
5 world-famous Olympic gold medallist and a sports adviser to government ministers.

At primary school Kelly tried dance and majorettes but did neither for
10 long. Then, when she was 12 and attending Hugh Christie School in Tonbridge, she was encouraged by teacher Debbie Page to do athletics. 'She was full of energy,
15 motivating and, most of all passionate,' recalls Kelly. 'She identified a talent in me and advised

20 me to take up athletics after I came second in a cross country race. I was the fastest in my class and in my school. I still hold some of my school records! I loved sport at school and was very lucky to have a great PE teacher.'

So she joined Tonbridge Athletics Club and started work with her first coach, Dave Arnold. She became the all England schools' 1500 metre champion when she was only 13, six months after she started running.

25 When she left school Kelly became an army driver and later became a physical training instructor and believes that it was the discipline she had learned in the army which worked in her favour later. At 22 she left the army, returned to athletics, trained hard and began to win.

She won a gold medal for the 1500 metre race in the 1994 Commonwealth
30 Games, for example, and repeated that success eight years later, having won a silver in 1998. She did well in the 1996 Olympic games in Atlanta too, but her finest moments were yet to come.

In 2000 Kelly won a bronze medal for the 800 metres at the Sydney Olympics. Then, in Athens in 2004 and at the age of 34, she won gold
35 medals for both the 800 and the 1500 metre races – a huge personal triumph and a tremendous sporting achievement for Britain to be proud of.

That is why, in 2005, she was made Dame of the British Empire – Dame Kelly Holmes – by the Queen. In the same year she won the Laureus World Sports Woman of the Year Award. And she lists no fewer than 16 other 'of
40 the year' awards on her website – including BBC sports personality of the year.

Since retiring from athletics, Kelly has worked hard as National School Sports Champion and visited many schools to promote the sport which she loved so much herself. She is advising the government about how to get
45 children doing more active sport in schools and is helping the Mayor of London with plans for the 2012 Olympics.

Susan Elkin

EXERCISE 10.2

Read the extract 'Running all the way to a gold medal' and answer the following questions in full sentences.

1. What is Kelly Holmes best known for?

2. In which year did she become all England schools' 1500 metre champion?

3. Which two people helped her most when she was still at school?

4. Where does Kelly Holmes think she learnt the discipline she needed?

5. How did the Queen acknowledge Kelly Holmes's achievements?

6. In what ways is Kelly Holmes well qualified for her current work?

7. Why do you think it's important to 'get children doing more active sport in schools'?

Your turn to write

EXERCISE 10.3

1. Write an account of a school match – any sport – for the school magazine.

2. Write a story entitled 'Goal'.

3. Write a story which includes the words 'I didn't think I'd ever win but …'.

4. Write a diary entry for someone who used to be a professional sportsman or woman a long time ago.

5. Write about sport in any way you wish.

6. Do you think there should be more or less sport played in schools? Why? Write your views.

✏ Improve your writing

EXERCISE 10.4

Write a paragraph explaining the principles of a sport (you choose which) for someone who knows nothing about it and has never seen it. Be as accurate and precise as you can. Keep it brief.

For example:

Table tennis is played by two players standing at either end of a large rectangular table. The object is to score points by hitting a lightweight small ball with a circular, short-handled bat over a low net across the middle of the table. Points are lost (gained by the opponent) if the ball played misses the table or is hit into the net, or by a player failing to return the ball. As in all racquet sports, the skill is to place the ball where the opponent cannot reach it. Table tennis can also be played as 'doubles' with two people at either end of the table.

'A Subaltern's Love Song'

This is one of John Betjeman's best known poems. A subaltern is a junior army officer and this poem is set in the 1920s or '30s when more people still lived in large country houses. Betjeman campaigned to stop Victorian buildings, which he loved, being demolished in the 1960s and '70s.

1   Miss J. Hunter Dunn, Miss J. Hunter Dunn,
    Furnish'd and burnish'd by Aldershot sun,
    What strenuous singles we played after tea,
    We in the tournament – you against me!
5   Love-thirty, love-forty, oh! weakness of joy,
    The speed of a swallow, the grace of a boy,
    With carefullest carelessness, gaily you won,
    I am weak from your loveliness, Joan Hunter Dunn.

Miss Joan Hunter Dunn, Miss Joan Hunter Dunn,
10 How mad I am, sad I am, glad that you won,
The warm-handled racket is back in its press,
But my shock-headed victor, she loves me no less.
Her father's euonymus[1] shines as we walk,
And swing past the summer-house, buried in talk,
15 And cool the verandah that welcomes us in
To the six-o'clock news and a lime-juice and gin.
The scent of the conifers, sound of the bath,
The view from my bedroom of moss-dappled path,
As I struggle with double-end evening tie,
20 For we dance at the Golf Club, my victor and I.
On the floor of her bedroom lie blazer and shorts,
And the cream-coloured walls are be-trophied with sports,
And westering, questioning settles the sun,
On your low-leaded window, Miss Joan Hunter Dunn.
25 The Hillman is waiting, the light's in the hall,
The pictures of Egypt are bright on the wall,
My sweet, I am standing beside the oak stair
And there on the landing's the light on your hair.
By roads "not adopted", by woodlanded ways,
30 She drove to the club in the late summer haze,
Into nine-o'clock Camberley, heavy with bells
And mushroomy, pine-woody, evergreen smells.
Miss Joan Hunter Dunn, Miss Joan Hunter Dunn,
I can hear from the car park the dance has begun,
35 Oh! Surrey twilight! importunate band!
Oh! strongly adorable tennis-girl's hand!
Around us are Rovers and Austins afar,
Above us the intimate roof of the car,
And here on my right is the girl of my choice,
40 With the tilt of her nose and the chime of her voice.
And the scent of her wrap, and the words never said,
And the ominous, ominous dancing ahead.
We sat in the car park till twenty to one
And now I'm engaged to Miss Joan Hunter Dunn.

John Betjeman (1941)

Note:
[1] A type of tree

EXERCISE 10.5

Read 'A Subaltern's Love Song' and answer the following questions in full sentences.

1. (a) What game have the narrator and Joan Hunter Dunn been playing in the afternoon? (b) Who won?

2. What do they both do before their evening commitment?

3. What is the evening commitment?

4. What make is the car they travel in and who drives it?

5. From when until when do they sit in the car?

6. In which English county is the golf club?

7. Summarise what you learn about Joan Hunter Dunn.

8. How can you tell that the author is in love with her?

 Discuss

EXERCISE 10.6

1. One of the many memorable things about this poem is that it appeals to all the senses: sight, touch, hearing, taste and smell. Work with a partner or a small group and find examples of each of these senses being referred to in the poem. What does all this tell you about the subaltern?

2. Betjeman almost always wrote in rhyme and used regular rhythm. This particular poem swings along because he begins with the rhythm of the tennis and uses it to establish a beat for the rest of the poem. It makes it very easy to learn by heart. You may also notice the assonance in the name Joan Hunter Dunn which gives it a poetic rhythm. It makes it flow like a little phrase in music. The repeated 'u' sound in the last two words drives the phrase forward like a pulse. It sounds like the rhythm of a horse galloping.

He also uses a lot of internal rhyme – rhymes within lines – as well as at the ends of lines: 'furnish'd and burnish'd', 'mad I am, sad I am, glad.'

The rhythm in this poem gives us four **strong beats** in each line:

> And **west**ering, **quest**ioning, **sett**les the **sun**
>
> A**round** us are **Ro**vers and **Aus**tins a**far**

Three sets of paired <u>lighter syllables</u> separate the strong beats:

> And **west**<u>er</u>ing, **quest**<u>ion</u>ing, **sett**<u>les</u> <u>the</u> **sun**
>
> A**round** <u>us</u> <u>are</u> **Ro**<u>vers</u> <u>and</u> **Aus**<u>tins</u> a**far**

The pattern of strong beats separated by light syllables in this poem makes it swing along like a tennis match.

Do you find Betjeman's use of rhyme and rhythm annoying in any way or does it work well for you? Try to explain why.

Explore poetry further

1.   Write one four-line verse (about anything you like) using exactly the same rhyme and rhythm which Betjeman uses in 'A Subaltern's Love Song'.

2.   Find and read some more of John Betjeman's poems.

3.   Look for, and read, other poems relating to sport such as 'Vitai Lampada' by Henry Newbolt, 'Goalkeeper with a Cigarette' by Simon Armitage and 'A Lay of the Links' by Arthur Conan Doyle.

Grammar and punctuation

Agreement of subject and verb

The pronouns 'I', 'he', 'she' and 'it'; words which end with 'one' (such as 'no one', 'none', 'anyone', 'everyone'); and words which end with 'body' (such as 'everybody', 'anybody', 'nobody' and 'somebody') are all **singular** words. Only one person or thing is involved.

The words 'we', 'they', 'people' and 'most' are **plural** words. More than one person or thing is involved.

Verbs must match – or agree with – the nouns to which they belong:

Singular	Plural
I was	We were
She was	They were
No one was	People were
Everybody was	All were
None is	Many are

EXERCISE 10.7

Put 'was' or 'were' into the gaps in this passage:

We _____ waiting for the bus. We didn't mind whether it _____ a red, green or blue bus. We _____ prepared to take the first one that came. The centre of town _____ our destination. My eldest sister _____ going to a wedding and she _____ planning to buy a really special outfit. Determined as she _____ to buy something extravagant and colourful, we _____ sure that she would buy something black and dreary, because that's what she always does. However, none of us _____ right.

She eventually chose a bright pink suit, which she _____ going to wear with a lime green blouse and scarlet hat. Everybody _____ trying to dissuade her, but unfortunately we _____ unsuccessful. She _____ all set to go to the wedding looking like a parrot.

Collective nouns

A collective noun is a group word such as 'team' or 'side', both of which mean a group of players in a sport. Words like 'flock' (of birds), 'pack' (of wolves or cards) and 'clutch' (of eggs in a nest) are collective nouns too.

You have to be especially careful with the verbs when you are using collective nouns. Collective nouns are **singular**.

You should write:

- The herd of cows was brown and white.
- Was the baseball team dressed in bright colours?
- The crowd was waving thousands of red, white and blue flags.

If, however, the subject is just 'cows', 'baseball players' or 'audience members', then these are **plural** because you are not using a collective noun. Remember: one team (singular); eleven players (plural).

EXERCISE 10.8

Match up these collective nouns with the common nouns to which they refer:

1. fleet   (a) singers
2. host   (b) bells
3. chest   (c) ships
4. swarm   (d) grapes
5. peal   (e) angels
6. gang   (f) insects
7. choir   (g) drawers
8. bunch   (h) thieves

EXERCISE 10.9

Write out these sentences using the right form of the verb (in the present tense):

1. The hockey team _____ triumphant after its win.
2. The hockey players _____ nervous about their match.
3. Everyone in the team _____ delighted.
4. The school's swimming relay team _____ looking forward to the gala.
5. _____ the musicians confident about the concert?
6. The wolf pack _____ howling.
7. The choir _____ on top form.
8. Everybody _____ pleased.

Semicolons

A semicolon (;) can be used to separate items in a list where the list is too complicated and the sentence too long for commas to be strong enough.

Look at this sentence:

- 'In our school we play football, hockey, tennis, cricket and rounders.'

This is correct (see Chapter 3).

But suppose that you want to add additional information about each sport within a single long sentence:

- In our school we play football, very popular with the boys, because we have extensive playing fields; hockey, loved by both boys and girls now that we have an all weather pitch; tennis, which works well because Mr Jonas, our tennis coach, is such an expert; cricket, although girls are not too keen; and rounders, which is a wonderful, all round game for pupils who aren't all that fond of sport.

The four semicolons are used to divide the main items on the list. Commas come between the semicolons to break up the additional information.

EXERCISE 10.10

Extend these sentences by giving more information about each of the sports mentioned, using semicolons:

1. My sister plays squash, badminton, tennis and table tennis.

2. The most popular sports on television are football, tennis, cricket and snooker.

3. I like swimming, ice-skating, ballet and riding.

Vocabulary and spelling

1. A **referee** (note the '-ee' at the end) is someone who is referred to for a decision in a sports match. An **employee** is someone who is employed. A **nominee** is someone who is nominated (named or chosen).

    New words (neologisms) are sometimes made up using patterns like these. For example, teachers now often refer to the pupils in their tutor group or form as **tutees**.

2. **Hemisphere** means half the world. It comes from the Greek words meaning 'half' and 'ball-shaped'. **Hemialgia** is pain limited to one side of the body and a **hemistitch** is half a line of verse. A **hemidemisemiquaver** is a musical term meaning half of a half of a half of a quaver.

You hold a hemidemisemiquaver for one sixty-fourth of a semibreve (a semibreve is four full beats); no wonder musicians are often also good at maths!

Check that you know the spellings of these words, all taken from the two passages which open this chapter:

confetti	medallist	disappeared	passionate
nineteenth	achievement	beckoning	disbelief
government	athletics		

To, two and too

Look carefully at these sentences:

- Rugby is one of **two** sports which are **too** good **to** miss.

- I know you are going **to** the **two** matches so can I come **too**?

- I want **to** play **two** games **too**.

Two: the number which comes between one and three

Too: an adverb meaning excess of something. It also means 'as well'

To: a place word (preposition) as in 'to the match'; part of a verb as in 'to miss'

EXERCISE 10.11

Write out these sentences putting **two**, **too** or **to** into the spaces:

1. Our first eleven beat Millford School by _____ goals _____ one.

2. It was _____ hot even _____ play tennis so we sat and ate _____ ice creams each.

3. _____ boys played _____ girls at table tennis in a game which the boys were surprised _____ lose.

4. Lacrosse is popular but lots of pupils like hockey _____.

5. I am going _____ work on cricketing skills this year, especially bowling.

6. My _____ friends and I have all been chosen _____ swim for the school.

> ## Speaking and listening

1. Find out about a sport that you have never played and know nothing about. Give a short talk to the class about its history, rules and how and where it is played.

2. Some adults think that sport, especially when it is played in teams, makes young people too competitive and is therefore not a good thing. Discuss this in a group. Try to consider all sides of the argument. Think of reasons why sport benefits young people and think of arguments against it.

3. Choose your favourite sport and then work with a partner who has chosen a different sport. Tell your partner about your favourite sport and why you like it. The sports could include dance, gymnastics and athletics. Listen very carefully to your partner. Then join up with another pair. Take turns to tell the other pair, not about your own, but about your partner's sport.

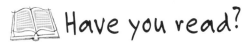 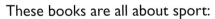

Have you read?

These books are all about sport:

- *Billy the Kid* by Michael Morpurgo (2000)
- *Goalkeepers are Different* by Brian Glanville (1971)
- *Down the Wicket* by Bob Cattell (2001)
- *Bend It Like Beckham* by Narinder Dhami (2002)
- *Ganging Up* by Alan Gibbons (1995)
- *Together on Ice* by Nicholas Walker (1994)
- *The Transfer* by Terence Blacker (1998)
- *Quidditch Through the Ages: Comic Relief Edition* by JK Rowling (2001)
- *Darcey Bussell's Favourite Ballet Stories* (2002)
- *Gala Star* by Ruth Dowley (2001)
- *One Good Horse* by Michael Hardcastle (1993)
- *Black, White and Gold* by Kelly Holmes (2005)
- *Football Fever* edited by Tony Bradman (1997)
- *A Book of Two Halves* edited by Nicholas Royle (1996)

✔ And if you've done all that ...

- Football Association teams often have mysterious names such as Sheffield Wednesday, Tottenham Hotspur, Wolverhampton Wanderers and so on. Do you know why Arsenal players are nicknamed 'the Gunners'? Find out how and when some of these teams got their names. The clubs themselves may help you if you contact them and/or there may be information on the internet.

- Research and write a short essay-length biography of a sporting hero or heroine from the past: WG Grace, Stanley Matthews, Roger Bannister, Kitty Godfrey – for example.

- In her Harry Potter books, JK Rowling devises Quidditch, a completely new sport for her young wizards and witches to play on broomsticks. Can you devise a fictional sport, complete with rules?

    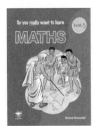
  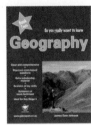  

   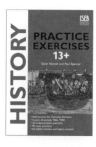 
    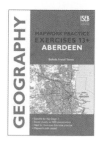

Galore Park
ISEB REVISION GUIDES

GALORE PARK

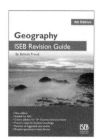

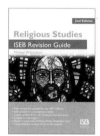

- All titles endorsed by the Independent Schools Examinations Board

- Perfect for 11+, 13+ and scholarship entrance exam preparation

- Consolidates the key subject information into ONE resource making revision a breeze!

- Enables pupils to identify gaps in knowledge to focus their revision

- Worked examples show pupils how to gain the best possible marks

- Each guide includes practice material and answers to test understanding

ISEB
Independent Schools
Examinations Board